W9-CSK-181

WASHINGTON, D.C.
SIGHTSEERS'
★ GUIDE ★

BY ANTHONY S. PITCH

Mino Publications, Inc.
Potomac, Maryland

ACKNOWLEDGMENTS

Cover photograph of the Capitol used with permission of the Architect of the Capitol.

Metrorail map, pages 8–9, and photograph, page 27, courtesy Washington Metropolitan Area Transit Authority.

All other photographs courtesy of Washington Convention & Visitors Association.

Published by

Mino Publications, Inc.
9009 Paddock Lane
Potomac, Md. 20854

Library of Congress Catalog Card No. 86-70380

ISBN 0-931719-04-6

Text copyright (c) 1986 by Anthony S. Pitch
Maps, except Metrorail, copyright (c) 1986 by Mino Publications, Inc.

Printed in the United States of America

For my children, Michael and Nomi,
to fuel their wonder at the world around them

Also by Anthony S. Pitch

Exclusively Washington Trivia
Exclusively Presidential Trivia
Exclusively First Ladies Trivia
Bazak Guide to Israel
Bazak Guide to Italy
Peace
Inside Zambia—And Out

Washington, D.C. Sightseers' Guide is available at special bulk purchase discounts for sale promotions, conventions, fund raisers or premiums.

For details, write to

Mino Publications, Inc.
9009 Paddock Lane
Potomac, Md. 20854

CONTENTS

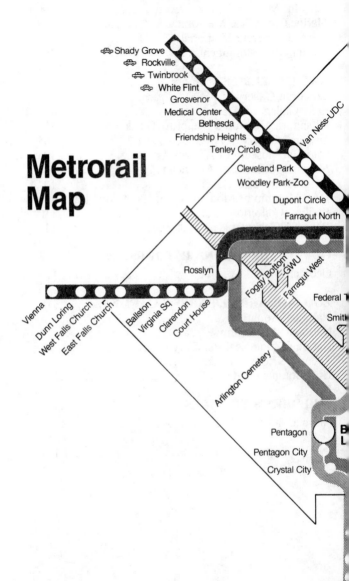

Metrorail Map

Shady Grove
Rockville
Twinbrook
White Flint
Grosvenor
Medical Center
Bethesda
Friendship Heights
Tenley Circle
Cleveland Park
Woodley Park-Zoo
Dupont Circle
Farragut North
Van Ness-UDC

Rosslyn
Foggy Bottom-GWU
Farragut West
Federal T
Smith

Vienna
Dunn Loring
West Falls Church
East Falls Church
Ballston
Virginia Sq
Clarendon
Court House

Arlington Cemetery

Pentagon
Pentagon City
Crystal City

B
L

8

YELLOW
LINE

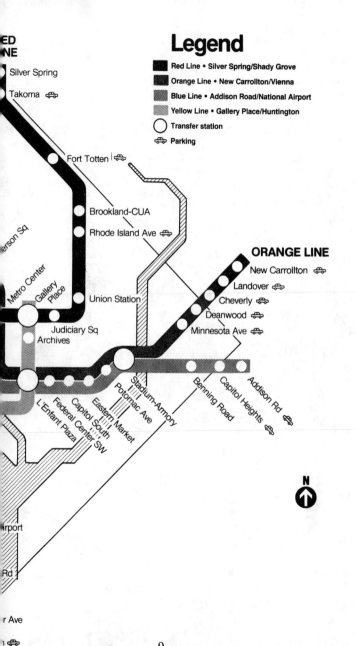

Silver Spring

Takoma

Legend

Red Line • Silver Spring/Shady Grove
Orange Line • New Carrollton/Vienna
Blue Line • Addison Road/National Airport
Yellow Line • Gallery Place/Huntington
Transfer station
Parking

Fort Totten

Brookland-CUA

Rhode Island Ave

erson Sq

Metro Center

Gallery Place

Union Station

ORANGE LINE

New Carrollton

Landover

Cheverly

Deanwood

Minnesota Ave

Judiciary Sq

Archives

Stadium-Armory

Potomac Ave

Eastern Market

Capitol South

Federal Center SW

L'Enfant Plaza

Benning Road

Capitol Heights

Addison Rd

N

irport

Rd

r Ave

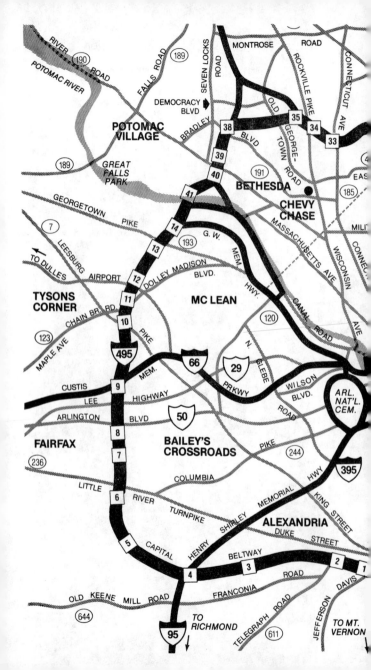

CAPITAL BELTWAY AND VICINITY

Published by Mino Publications, Inc. ©1986
9009 Paddock Lane • Potomac, Maryland 20854

WELCOME!

Physically it is the most un-American of major U.S. cities. There are no skyscrapers, no smog and little dirt. It's lush green and expansive. Washingtonians fly kites and play weekend polo and baseball on the soft turf of the Mall in the shadow of the Capitol. There is almost a provincial ease about it.

A placid, pastoral city? Hardly! A drive up embassy row on Massachusetts Avenue, past the multi-colored flags of foreign embassies, reinforces a visual awareness of being in the world's foremost capital.

Less obvious is the Washington which churns with the currents of all manner of power brokers. There are legions of lawyers, lobbyists and legislators. This is, after all, the citadel of prestige. And for those elected or driven to lead and influence, Washington is nothing less than the end of the rainbow.

But the Federal capital is also a beguiling city of glamor and glitter, with moments of sheer magic. Times have changed since Walt Whitman saw Abraham Lincoln ride a gray horse through the streets of Washington, and observed "only some curious stranger stops and gazes." More than a hundred years later strangers expect Washington to provide events out of the ordinary and celebrities larger than life.

Few go home disappointed. You may sense a stir downtown as police momentarily halt traffic. Sirens wail as motorcycle outriders flank a cavalcade of cars. Bystanders stop to catch a fleeting glimpse of the prominent figure. It is none other than the President of the United States. Long after his limousine has sped by, sensations remain heightened. Such is the recurring spell that Washington casts over so many visitors.

But Washington is far from being overwhelmed by the powerful and the socially prominent. The flowering of the Tidal Basin's Japanese cherry trees in the first weeks of spring is awaited more eagerly than any Fourth of July fireworks show or presidential inaugural parade down Pennsylvania Avenue. To be in Washington during these precious few weeks is to see the capital in the prime of its seasonal change. In this moment of time it is ravishing, and no single personality can hope to compete for attention.

FREE TOURIST INFORMATION & PAMPHLETS

Up-to-date information of special use to sightseers can be obained from the following offices:

Washington Convention & Visitors' Association
1575 Eye St. N.W. Suite #250
Tel: 789-7000
Open: Mon.–Fri. 9 a.m.–5 p.m.

Washington Tourist Information Center
Department of Commerce Building,
Pennsylvania Ave., between 14th & 15th Streets N.W.
Tel: 789-7000
Open: Apr. 6–Sept. 28 daily 9 a.m.–5 p.m.
        Sept. 29–Apr. 5 Mon.–Sat. 9 a.m.–5 p.m.

International Visitors Information Service
733 15th St. N.W. (between H St. & New York Ave.)
Tel: 783-6540
Open: Mon.–Fri. 9 a.m.–5 p.m.

National Park Service
Public Affairs Department
1100 Ohio Drive S.W.
Tel: 426-6700
Open: Mon.–Fri. 8 a.m.–4 p.m.

D.C. Chamber of Commerce
1341 G St. N.W. (at 14th St.) Suite #312
Tel: 347-7202
Open: Mon.–Fri. 8:30 a.m.–5:30 p.m.

EMBASSIES

Australia	1601 Massachusetts Ave. N.W.	797-3000
Austria	2343 Massachusetts Ave. N.W.	483-4474
Belgium	3330 Garfield St. N.W.	333-6900
Brazil	3006 Massachusetts Ave. N.W.	745-2700
Canada	2450 Massachusetts Ave. N.W.	483-5505
China	2300 Connecticut Ave. N.W.	328-2500
Denmark	3200 Whitehaven St. N.W.	234-4300
Egypt	2310 Decatur Place N.W.	232-5400
Finland	3216 New Mexico Ave. N.W.	363-2430
France	4101 Reservoir Rd. N.W.	944-6000
Germany	4645 Reservoir Rd. N.W.	298-4000
Great Britain	3100 Massachusetts Ave. N.W.	462-1340
Greece	2221 Massachusetts Ave. N.W.	667-3168
India	2107 Massachusetts Ave. N.W.	939-7000
Ireland	2234 Massachusetts Ave. N.W.	462-3939
Israel	3514 International Drive N.W.	364-5500
Italy	1601 Fuller St. N.W.	328-5500
Japan	2520 Massachusetts Ave. N.W.	234-2266
Luxembourg	2200 Massachusetts Ave. N.W.	265-4171
Mexico	2829 16th St. N.W.	234-6000
Netherlands	4200 Linnean Ave. N.W.	244-5300
New Zealand	37 Observatory Circle N.W.	328-4800
Norway	2720 34th St. N.W.	333-6000
Pakistan	2315 Massachusetts Ave. N.W.	939-6200
Philippines	1617 Massachusetts Ave. N.W.	483-1414
Portugal	2310 Tracy Place N.W.	328-8610
Saudi Arabia	601 New Hampshire Ave. N.W.	342-3800
Singapore	1824 R. St. N.W.	667-7555
South Africa	3051 Massachusetts Ave. N.W.	232-4400
Spain	2700 15th St. N.W.	265-0190
Sweden	600 New Hampshire Ave. N.W.	298-3500
Switzerland	2900 Cathedral Ave. N.W.	745-7900
UAE	600 New Hampshire Ave. N.W.	338-6500
U.S.S.R.	1125 16th St. N.W.	628-7551

IMPORTANT TELEPHONE NUMBERS

Emergencies

Police: 911
Fire: 911
Ambulance: 911
U.S. Park Police: 426-6680
Medical Referral Service: 466-1880
Dental Referral Service: 686-0803
Members of Congress: 224-3121

What's On

Visitor Information Center: 789-7000
International Visitors Information Service: 783-6540
Convention & Visitors' Association: 789-7000
Daily Tourist Information: 737-8866
Dial-a-Museum Information: 357-2020
Dial-a-Park Information: 426-6975
National Park Service Information: 426-6700
Smithsonian Museums Information: 357-2700
White House Tour Information: 456-7041
Zoo Information: 673-4800

Transportation:

American Automobile Association: 331-3000
Amtrak Trains: 484-7540
Gray Line Bus Tours: 479-5900
Metrorail/Metrobus Information: 637-7000
Metrorail/Metrobus Handicapped Service: 962-1245
Taxi Information/Complaints: 727-5401
Tourmobile: 554-7950

Parking Violations

Fines for booting/tow away: 727-5000
Repossession of towed vehicle: 576-6585

HISTORY

In 1791 George Washington chose the site for what he called the Federal City. It was to be 100 square miles of land ceded by Maryland and Virginia. The area included the ports of Alexandria and Georgetown.

Washington chose a Frenchman to plan the city. Major Pierre L'Enfant, who had fought in the Revolutionary War, drew up grandiose plans for a grid of streets cut across by boulevards and intersected by fountains and statuary. But once in charge, L'Enfant rode roughshod over other's feelings. Within a year he was fired. However, his basic plan survives.

When the government moved from Philadelphia to the new capital in 1800, Abigail Adams, wife of President John Adams, agonized over the primitive conditions. Washington, she wrote, was a city "only so in name."

Fourteen years later, British redcoats burned many of the buildings, including the White House and Capitol, in the last war between the two countries.

The city's growth, bedevilled by mosquito-infested swamps, was slow. Charles Dickens poked fun at Washington's appearance during a visit in 1842. "Washington consists of spacious avenues that begin in nothing and lead nowhere; streets, mile-long, that only want houses, roads and inhabitants; public buildings that need but a public to be complete."

Diplomatic postings to Washington were accompanied by hardship allowances. An exasperated French diplomat cried: "Mon Dieu! What have I done to be condemned to reside in such a city!"

By 1846 Virginians were so disgusted at having ceded Alexandria to the city of Washington that they drummed up enough support for its return.

Then, flamboyant Alexander "Boss" Shepherd took charge as head of the newly-created board of

The Washington Monument

public works. He paved streets, laid sewers, planted trees and filled in the bogs of Tiber Creek.

Monumental construction continues. Below ground, the Metrorail lines press further into Virginia and Maryland to serve commuters. And the city's new massive Convention Center is within walking distance of the White House.

Today the city's population stands at about 630,000.

Pierre L'Enfant would indeed be proud.

ORIENTATION

The boundaries of the District of Columbia look like a diamond resting in such a way that its points face north, east and south. The Potomac River forming the western side washes so far in that it makes the diamond imperfect.

The entire area is divided into four sections. They are formed by the intersection of North Capitol Street, South Capitol Street, East Capitol Street and the Mall, to the west. The U.S. Capitol is at the center of this intersection.

The four sections make up northwest, northeast, southwest and southeast Washington. Whenever a Washington, D.C. address is given it is always followed by the abbreviation of the section it is in—N.W., N.E., S.W., or S.E.

Streets running north and south are numbered, beginning with 1st Street N.E., both of which are closest to the Capitol.

Streets going east and west are named after letters of the alphabet. There is no J Street. West of the Capitol there are also no A or B Streets. Independence Avenue takes the place of B Street in southwest and southeast, and Constitution Avenue substitutes for B Street in northwest and northeast.

Streets which run diagonally are invariably named after U.S. States. A section of the most prominent one is the presidential inaugural route along Pennsylvania Avenue N.W., from the Capitol, past the Visitor Information Center at the junction of 14th Street N.W., to the White House.

The Mall cuts a grassy green swathe from the Capitol, west to the Reflecting Pool in front of the Lincoln Memorial. Slicing across this imaginery line drawn straight as a builder's level from the Capitol to the Lincoln Memorial, is another line of landmarks: the White House in the north and the Jefferson

Memorial in the south. Between them, but fractionally unaligned due to the swamps which once oozed here, is the Washington Monument.

The eastern half of the Mall, between the Capitol and 14th Street N.W., is lined with the world-renowned Smithsonian Institution Museums. Downtown parades and processions, including the annual Cherry Blossom Festival Parade in April, go down Constitution Avenue N.W., the northern perimeter of the Mall.

The most elegant downtown fashion shops are on the stretch of Connecticut Avenue N.W., overlooked by the venerably regal Mayflower Hotel, between Dupont Circle and Farragut Square.

K Street N.W., which intersects this portion of Connecticut Avenue, is where many of the city's legendary rainmakers—big-name lawyers who attract big-moneyed clients—have their plush offices. Here, too, are the carpeted havens of some of the highest-priced political consultants. Watching over them all is the Washington bureau of the New York Times.

The best bird's-eye-view of the downtown area can be had from atop the Observatory Tower of the Pavilion at the Old Post Office, corner of Pennsylvania Avenue and 12th Street N.W. The view from the top of the Washington Monument stretches, on a clear day, far into neighboring Virginia and Maryland.

Urban renewal has been so unrelenting since 1980 that the cityscape is undergoing a radical metamorphosis. Before the decade is out the run-down acreage centering around the sprawling Convention Center at 9th and H Streets N.W. will have been razed and modernized with shops, offices and top-flight hotels.

The modest size of the city's Chinatown, just east of the Convention Center, still boasts the largest number of pre-Civil War buildings between the Capitol and Georgetown. But even here the wrecker's ball has brought change, beginning with the new Metrorail station of Gallery Place, on the Yellow line.

HOW TO GET AROUND

GRAY LINE SIGHTSEEING TOURS

There is no better way of seeing the major sites of Washington, D.C. if you feel like being pampered in plush motorcoaches with expert guides.

Gray Line's regularly scheduled half-day and full-day tours cover the downtown area and immediate environs across the Potomac River. The fleet of coaches even reaches into distant parts of Virginia and New Jersey, operating day excursions to the casinos of Atlantic City, N.J. and one or three-day cruises into historic Williamsburg and other colonial towns.

A quickie two-hour observation tour of Washington covers Capitol Hill, the Pentagon, the major monuments and Embassy Row.

On the morning drive around Washington you stop for tours inside the White House—if it is open to visitors that day—at Ford's Theater, where President Lincoln was shot, at the Jefferson Memorial and the Museum of American History.

An afternoon outing includes a guided tour of the Capitol, the Air & Space Museum and a look at the Declaration of Independence inside the National Archives.

Of special appeal to budget-minded sightseers is Gray Line's year-round, three hour tour of Washington after dark.

The Black Heritage Tour, available to charter groups, takes in such landmarks as the home of abolitionist leader Frederick Douglass, the birthplace of "Duke" Ellington, and the campus of Howard University.

Other tours embrace Arlington National Cemetery and Mt. Vernon.

Gray Line has a courtesy pick-up service at many hotels. Further information is available from hotel concierges or front desks at most hotels, or by calling Gray Line direct at 479-5900. The terminal is at 333 E. Street S.W., a block southwest of the Federal Center Metro station on the Blue or Orange lines.

TOURMOBILE

The National Park Service granted this company a preferential right to provide tourist shuttle services to 18 major attractions, most along the Mall and Capitol areas and a handful across the Potomac River.

The shuttles, hitched together, stop at designated spots every 30 minutes. Sightseers can get on and off the fleet of trams at their own convenience. For example, you may take a shuttle to the Lincoln Memorial, get off and look around in your own good time, then catch another shuttle to your next destination site.

Tickets allow you to get on and off at your leisure, any number of times on the same day you bought your ticket.

Tickets may be purchased from the drivers or at kiosks next to some of the sites visited. Children under 11 are half price. Shuttles run between the hours of 9:30 a.m. and 4:30 p.m.

TAXIS

Washington, D.C. is divided into zones to calculate the base fare charged by taxis. A zone map must be displayed in every taxi.

Transportation within the same zone is cheaper than crossing the line into another zone.

Surcharges are made for travel during rush hours, 6:30–9 a.m. and 4–6:30 p.m.

Additional charges are levied for more than one passenger, who is allowed only one free piece of baggage.

For further information, or complaints, telephone 727-5401.

BUSES

Metrobuses are not as fast, nor as punctual as Metrorail. We do not recommend them to sightseers upset by unwashed windows and seats scrawled with graffiti.

Visitors steeled to this sordid side of modern inner-city transportation, should know that exact change must be given to the driver on entering the bus. Make sure you have a supply of quarters, dimes and nickles adding up to at least one dollar.

Discounted *Flash Passes,* good for unlimited rides during fortnightly periods, obviate the need to carry small change. You have only to show the driver your *Flash Pass.*

These *Flash Passes* may be purchased at Metro headquarters, 5th & G. Streets, N.W. Mon.–Fri. 8 a.m.–4 p.m., at the Metro sales and information office inside Metro Center Station, 12th & F. Streets, N.W., Mon.–Fri. 7 a.m.–7 p.m., or at any Washington, D.C. branch of First American Bank.

For further information on routes or fares telephone 637-7000.

PARKING

The capital is no different from other major cities plagued by too many vehicles scrambling for limited parking space. The position worsens on Capitol Hill, where most of the streets closest to the Capitol, Supreme Court and Library of Congress have parking bays reserved for Congress members and their staffs.

Coin-operated meter parking operates Mon.–Fri. 9 a.m.–5 p.m. The downtown rate is 25¢ for every 20 minutes, with a maximum of two hours. Some streets have one-hour only parking meters.

Be careful to read the white signs stamped with instructions in red or green. In some areas it is forbidden to park during rush-hours only, 7–9:30 a.m. and 4–6:30 p.m.

It's no use scanning the vicinity for traffic officials carrying pads of parking violation tickets. They are among the most unobtrusive and vigilant city employees and are not given to merciful treatment just because you have out-of-town license plates.

The fines are stiff. Try easing into an empty taxi stand in front of one of the Smithsonian museums on the Mall and you'll be slapped with a $50 fine.

If your car is *booted* with a metal clasp on the wheel, it's officialdom's way of telling you to jump to it and pay outstanding fines. In this case, grab your money and rush to the Bureau of Traffic Adjudication, 1111 E. Street, N.W. It is open Mon.–Fri. 8:30 a.m.–7 p.m., Sat. 8:30 a.m.–12:30 p.m. Tel. 727-5000.

Your car may even be towed away if you've neglected to pay fines and it's booted. It may also be towed if it's in a tow-away area or is interferring with rush-hour traffic. In this event, go first to pay the fine at the Bureau of Traffic Adjudication (see address above). Then take your receipt and driver's license to Brentwood Impoundment Lot at 1100 Brentwood Road, N.E. (next to the Rhode Island Metro station on the Red line). It is open Mon.–Fri. 7 a.m.–8 p.m., Sat. 8 a.m.–2 p.m., Tel. 576-6585. Your vehicle will be released only after proof of payment of the fine.

METRORAIL

The Washington Metrorail (mainly underground high-speed electrified train transport) is not only clean, comfortable and safe. It is perhaps the most attractive in the nation. In 1983 the American Institute of Architects awarded this urban mass transit system the prestigious Institute Honor for architectural design.

Of greater importance to tourists and visitors, Metrorail is also the quickest way of traveling through downtown Washington, D.C. and between the outlying suburbs in Maryland and Virginia.

Most of the 60 miles of lines run underground, though sections, notably the Yellow line across the Potomac River, provide scenic views.

Metro was opened in 1976 and now serves 60 stations. The rail cars were bought from Breda Costruzioni Ferroviarie in Italy.

It is forbidden to smoke, eat or drink, or to play radios or tape recorders on the Metro.

HOURS OF OPERATION: Mon.–Fri. 6 a.m.–midnight; Sat. 8 a.m.–midnight; Sun. 10 a.m.–6 p.m.; Arlington Cemetery station closes at 7 p.m. from the last Sunday in October through the last Sunday in April. *Holiday Schedule:* New Year's Day: 10 a.m.–6 p.m.; Martin Luther King Jr's Birthday and Washington's Birthday: 6:30 a.m.–midnight; Memorial Day: 10 a.m.–6 p.m.; Independence Day: check special schedule; Labor Day: 10 a.m.–6 p.m.; Columbus Day: 6:30 a.m.–midnight; Veterans' Day: 6:30 a.m.–midnight; Thanksgiving Day: 10 a.m.–6 p.m; Christmas Day: 10 a.m.–6 p.m.

DISABLED PERSONS: All Metrorail stations have elevators to take on wheelchairs. Special I.D. cards for handicapped persons, entitling them to discounted farecards, are available upon application to the Washington Metropolitan Area Transit Authority headquarters at 600 Fifth Street, N.W., Washington, D.C. 20001, Mon., Thurs., Fri. 8 a.m.–4:30 p.m, and on the 2nd Sat. 11 a.m.–noon with prior reservations (or telephone Handicap Information 962-1245).

GOING BY METRO: Just before the faregates inside every Metro station, you'll see large colored maps of the rapid rail system, enclosed in backlighted glass display cases.

One of the maps shows a detailed section of the neighborhood served by each station. The other map traces the rail system's Red, Orange, Blue and Yellow

Courtesy Washington Metropolitan Area Transit Authority

Metrorail Station

lines which operate between Washington, D.C. and the suburbs in Maryland and Virginia.

SELECT YOUR DESTINATION STATION: Having identified your destination station, note the color of the line. Take care to determine whether you have to transfer during the ride onto another line, and if so, identify the name of the transfer station.

WHAT DOES IT COST?: Look to the lower portion of the maps. Destination stations are listed alphabetically. Opposite each are two columns of varying prices. Fares are determined by distance traveled and whether it is rush hour or non-rush hour. Rush hours are Mon. through Fri. 6 a.m.–9:30 p.m. and 3 p.m.–6:30 p.m. Children under 5 ride free if accompanied by a paying passenger (maximum of 2 children per paying passenger).

BUYING A FARECARD: Move to the adjacent farecard vending machines. Each Metrorail rider requires a separate farecard. These machines take coins or $1 and $5 bills.

There are three easy steps to buying the farcard:

1. Begin at the left hand side on the face of the machine. Coins are dropped into the vertical slot. Bills must be inserted face up, with Washington's face ($1) or Lincoln's portrait ($5) look-

ing to your left. Badly wrinkled or crumpled bills will be rejected by the machine. If you plan on taking a number of Metro rides you may wish to buy a card with a value of at least $10 to earn the 5% bonus.

2. In the middle section, under *Farecard Value,* you'll see white buttons. Both the dollar and cent buttons have + and − signs. If your farecard costs less than the amount of money you deposited, press the − button gently until it matches the fare required. If you accidentally allowed the amount shown to go below the fare, press the + sign to adjust it.

3. The farecard can now be received by pressing the white button on the right hand side of the face of the machine.

COLLECT YOUR CHANGE!: Don't forget to collect any change due to you. This drops into the container inside the lower left portion of the machine at the same moment that you press the button for your farecard.

GETTING YOUR MONEY BACK: If you decide to trade in your farecard to regain fare money unused, place the card in the slot below the one where your farecard came out.

USING THE FAREGATES: Walk to the faregates. The green light with a white arrow should be on the right of your faregate. Insert the farecard face up, with the arrow pointed forward, into the slot in the beveled front of the console.

The card is automatically encoded with the name of the station and the time that you entered the faregate.

If there is insufficient money marked on the card, the faregate will not open and the station attendant should be called.

The encoded farecard now comes up through a slot on top of the console while the gate opens.

Take the farecard with you but do not fold, wrinkle, tear or wet it. The farecard's magnetic strip holds the card's value. If the strip is demagnetized the card loses all value.

BUS TRANSFERS: Now is the time to get a bus transfer ticket if you need a bus to complete your trip from your destination station. The free transfers are obtained by pressing the button on machines at the top of escalators going down to Metrorail platforms. These tickets are good for a free bus ride in D.C. to complete your journey, and for discounts on tickets for trips out of Washington.

AT THE DESTINATION STATION: At the destination station repeat the procedure at the faregate. The console deducts the fare and prints the remaining value on your card. If your farecard had the exact amount for the ride just taken, the console will not return the farecard to you after the gate opens.

ADDFARE: If the value of the farecard is insufficient for the ride, a sign will light up on the console, barring your exit. Go back to the Addfare machine. Insert your card. The Additional Farecard display will advise you of the shortfall. Insert the balance owing and Addfare will return your farecard, together with any change due.

HANDY HINT: Avoid delays, especially during rush hours, by purchasing high value farecards up to the maximum of $20. This way you will not have to wait in line at the farecard vendor each time.

IMPORTANT METRO TELEPHONE NUMBER: Information, Bus or Rail 637-7000

CALENDAR OF ANNUAL EVENTS

Exact dates and times of many of these events should be checked beforehand at the *Visitor Information Center,* Pennsylvania Ave., between 14th & 15th Streets N.W. tel. 789-7000. Open: April 6–September 28, seven days a week 9 a.m.–5 p.m., September 29–April 5, Mon.-Sat. 9 a.m.–5 p.m. You may also check with the *Washington, D.C. Convention and Visitors Association,* 1575 Eye Street N.W. tel. 789-7000 and the *National Park Service,* Office of Public Affairs, tel. 426-6700. Daily events are also provided on a recording, tel. 737-8866.

JANUARY

Martin Luther King, Jr's Birthday (3rd Monday): Speeches, dance, choral performances throughout the Washington metropolitan area in honor of the civil rights leader. Information, tel. 755-1005

U.S. Army Band Annual Anniversary Concert: Musical and choral selections in a free concert a D.A.R. Constitution Hall. Information, tel. 692-7219

FEBRUARY

Black History Month: Museum exhibits, cultural programs and special events to emphasize black contribution to U.S. history. Information, tel. 357-2700

Abraham Lincoln's Birthday (February 12): Wreath-laying ceremony and recitation of the Gettysburg Address at the Lincoln Memorial. Free. Information, tel. 426-6700

George Washington's Birthday (Monday before Feb. 22): Open house at his estate, Mt. Vernon, Va. Also wreath-laying ceremony and posting of colors by joint military honor guard at Washington Monument. tel. 426-6700.

Chinese New Year's Festival: Firecrackers and dragon dancers in Chinatown's decorated streets close to the Convention Center. Information, tel. 231-5411

MARCH

St. Patrick's Day Parade: Parade along Constitution Avenue N.W. with bands, floats, dancers. Information, tel. 424-2200

Easter Egg Roll At White House: Traditional Easter Egg roll on White House lawns for children under 8 accompanied by adults. Eggs provided. Also entertainment. Information, tel. 456-2200

Smithsonian Kite Festival: Prizes and trophies for all ages of kite flyers who gather on Washington Monument grounds. Free. Information, tel. 357-3030

APRIL

Cherry Blossom Festival (early April): Week-long celebration of flowering Japanese Cherry trees ringing the Tidal Basin in front of the Jefferson Memorial. Lighting of Japanese stone lantern, lunch-time concerts downtown, fashion shows, dances, boat races climaxed by 3-hour parade along Constitution Avenue N.W. with floats, bands, drill teams. Information, tel. 293-0480 or 426-6700

Thomas Jefferson's Birthday (April 13): Wreath-laying ceremony at Jefferson Memorial. Information, tel. 426-6700

Georgetown Garden Tour: Full-day tour of private gardens of about a dozen homeowners, some celebrities, in aid of a day-care center for children of low-income working parents. Admission fee, depending when booked. Information, tel. 333-4953 or 338-4229

Georgetown House Tour: Tour of about a dozen elegant, historic and architecturally unique private homes over two days, each day noon–5 p.m. Tickets include high tea. Sponsored by St. John's Episcopal Church. Information, tel. 338-1796

D.C. School Safety Patrol Parade: Marching bands, cheerleaders, majorettes, floats and drum and bugle corps parade down Constitution Avenue N.W. Information, tel. 636-4225

Gross National Parade: High jinks, unorthodox parade benefiting Police Boys and Girls Club of D.C. More than 100,000 spectators. From near White House to Georgetown. Information, tel. 686-3051

White House Spring Garden Tour: Tour includes the Jacqueline Kennedy Rose Garden and the West Lawn. Information, tel. 456-2200

Smithsonian's Washington Craft Show: One-of-a-kind arts and crafts sales exhibition. Exhibitors selected by panel of experts. Works in ceramics, glass, jewelry, leather, metal, paper, textiles, wood, Admission. Information, tel. 357-4000

William Shakespeare's Birthday: Music, theater, children's events, food and exhibits at Folger Shakespeare Library. On Saturday closest to his April 23 birthday, the Tudor banqueting hall is open to public. Information, tel. 544-7077

MAY

Tour of Foreign Embassies: A look around some half dozen embassies. Tickets, to benefit Davis Memorial Goodwill Industries, include shuttle bus service between embassies, and tea. Information, tel. 636-4225

National Tourism Week: Many civic and other events tie in with the nation's celebration of the travel and tourism industry. Information, tel. 293-1433 or 789-7007

Memorial Day (last Monday in May): Wreath-laying at Tomb of Unknown Soldier in Arlington National Cemetery and at Vietnam Veterans Memorial. Information, tel. 426-6700. National Symphony Orchestra has evening performance on west lawn of Capitol. Information, tel. 475-0843

ALL SUMMER LONG

Courtyard Concert Series (May–September): Rock, jazz, pop and military bands, including some from Europe and Canada, perform at the FBI building, 9th St. & Pennsylvania Ave. N.W. noon–1 p.m. Information, tel. 324-5348

U.S. Military Band Concerts (June–August): At 8 p.m. at Sylvan Theater near Washington Monument, Sun., Tues., Thurs., Fri. At west terrace of U.S. Capitol on Mon., Tues., Wed., Fri. Information, tel. 426-6700.

Sunday Polo (May–October): Sunday afternoon matches at Lincoln Memorial field. May, 2 p.m., June, 3 p.m., July–August, 4 p.m., September–October, 3 p.m. Free. Information, tel. 426-6700

C & O Canal Barge Rides (Apr.–Oct.): Mule-drawn barges pulled up scenic Chesapeake & Ohio Canal. Costumed Park Service guides on each trip. Depart from 30th & Jefferson Streets, N.W. in Georgetown. Admission. Information, tel. 472-4376

JUNE

Marine Band Summer Concerts: Outdoor concerts on west steps of Capitol, Wednesdays. At Sylvan Theater, near Washington Monument, Sundays. Information, tel. 433-4011

Potomac Riverfest: Two days of free entertainment, tall ships, arts & crafts, fireworks, boat rides, water events, ethnic foods at Potomac riverside. Information, tel. 387-8292

Spirit of America Concert: Military bands trace the history of America through music and skits. At Capital Centre, Landover, Md. Information, tel. 696-3147.

Fourth of July fireworks over Washington

National Zoo Summerfest: Musicians and dancers entertain with jazz, modern dance, bluegrass, classical music and mime outdoors. Information, tel. 673-4717

Wianki Festival of the Wreaths: 6 p.m. picnic at Lincoln Memorial followed by music and dance. Candles lit on flowered wreaths in the Reflecting Pool to celebrate the summer solstice. Information, tel. 656-3592

Festival of American Folklife: Performances and demonstrations on Mall of traditional music, crafts, and other folk heritage. Ethnic foods. Information, tel. 357-2700

JULY

Cracker Jack Old Timers Baseball Classic (early June–late July): Five-inning contest between old timers of the American League and the National League, at RFK Memorial Stadium. Admission. Information, tel. 544-5550

Independence Day Celebrations (Fourth of July): Free concert on Washington Monument grounds, normally attracts hundreds of thousands. Evening fireworks display. Also National Symphony Orchestra performs on west steps of Capitol. Information, tel. 426-6700

Twilight Tattoo: By 3rd U.S. Infantry Old Guard. Wednesdays on Ellipse at 7 p.m. Information, tel. 696-3147.

Latin American Festival: Latino community of Adams-Morgan and Mt. Pleasant areas celebrate with week-long arts & crafts and food for sale, and plays, music and dance. Information, tel. 328-6533

AUGUST

Navy Band Lollipop Concert: U.S. Navy Band presents special program for children of all ages at the

The Kennedy Center

Sylvan Theater, next to Washington Monument. Free. Information, tel. 433-6090

SEPTEMBER

Labor Day Concert (Labor Day weekend): Final outdoor summer concert by National Symphony Orchestra on west lawn of Capitol. Information, tel. 785-8100

Redskins Football Season Opens: The Washington Redskins play their season opener in another quest for Super Bowl glory. RFK Stadium. Information, tel. 546-2222

Constitution Day: The original of the U.S. Constitution is displayed in its entirety at the National Archives on this anniversary of its signing. Information, tel. 523-3216

Rock Creek Park Day: Birthday celebrations for Washington's largest park celebrated with musical entertainment, food, arts & crafts, exhibits and demonstrations. Information, tel. 426-6832

OCTOBER

Columbus Day (2nd Monday): Mass at the National Shrine of the Immaculate Conception. Also Italian cultural exhibits, military band concert. Wreath-laying at Columbus Memorial at Union Station. Information, tel. 638-0220

International Urban Fair: Three-day celebration with jazz, reggae music, food and parade from Rhode Island Ave. N.E. to District Building at Pennsylvania Ave. N.W. Information, tel. 387-7990

White House Garden Tour: Includes the Rose Garden, south lawn and music by a military band. Information, tel. 426-6700 or 472-3669

U.S. Navy Band Birthday Concert: Birthday concert of U.S. Navy Band at D.A.R. Constitution Hall. Free tickets must be picked up before the concert. Information, tel. 433-6090

NOVEMBER

Bullets Basketball Season Opens: The Washington Bullets play their season opener at the Capital Centre, Landover, Md. Information, tel. 350-3400

Washington's Review of Troops: Reenactment of George Washington's final review of his troops in front of Gadsby's Tavern, 138 N. Royal St. Alexandria, Va. Information, tel. 549-0205

Veterans' Day: Wreath-laying by President of U.S. or other top official at Tomb of the Unknown Soldier, Arlington National Cemetery, and at Vietnam Veterans Memorial. Information, tel. 426-6700

Armistice Day Commemoration: Special tour of the home of President Woodrow Wilson, with music of World War 1 period. Information, tel. 673-4034

DECEMBER

Scottish Christmas Walk: Alexandria, Va. celebrates its Scottish heritage with a parade through Old Town of bagpipers, highland dancers and bands. Information, tel. 549-0111 or 549-SCOT

Christmas Candlelight Tour: Colonial dancing and music during tour of Alexandria, Va.'s famous old homes, including the boyhood home of Robert E. Lee. Information, tel. 549-0205

Christmas Tree Lighting: Lighting of Christmas tree at Capitol with performance by military bands. Information, tel. 224-3069

Lighting of National Christmas Tree: Lit by President of the U.S. at the Ellipse, followed by nightly choral performances and display of Christmas trees representing every U.S. State, through New Year's Day. Information, tel. 426-6700

Chanukah Festival: Traditional food and holiday music at B'nai B'rith Klutznick Museum. Information, tel. 857-6583

Christmas Trees at the Smithsonian: Christmas trees, decorated and lit, on display in Museum of American History. Information, tel. 357-2700

Kwanzaa Celebration: Afro-American harvest festival, celebrating family life and unity. Anacostia Neighborhood Museum and Museum of African Art. Information, tel. 287-3369

New Year's Eve Celebration: Tens of thousands of celebrants gather at the site of the Old Post Office, Pennsylvania Ave. and 12th St. N.W. for entertainment and merrymaking. Information, tel. 289-4224

MUSEUMS

The Smithsonian "Castle" on The Mall

Anderson House

2118 Massachusetts Ave. N.W. between 21st & 22nd Sts.

Tel: 785-0540. Open: Tue.–Sat. 1–4 p.m. **Admission:** Free. **Metro station:** Dupont Circle on Red line.

Not even the price tag of $800,000 for this turn-of-the-century downtown residence prepares a visitor for the awesome sumptuousness of its fabled furnishings. It was the home of Larz Anderson, Minister to Belgium and Ambassador to Japan, and his wife, Isabel Weld Perkins, the Boston heiress. The remains of both are interred in Washington Cathedral.

You are barely in the front door when you catch your breath at the sight of a line of carved Italian Renaissance choir stalls. Gracing the regal dining room are woven 17th century Flemish tapestries, a gift from French King Louis XIII to the Papal representative to his court.

A doorway is an *open sesame* to the grand ballroom, fully 80 ft. long with a ceiling almost half as high. Parquet flooring leads to four twirling columns of antique Verona marble supporting the Musicians' Gallery. A gothic niche at gallery level contains the oldest object in the mansion—a 2000-year-old Chinese urn.

There is a paneled library, French and English parlors, a solarium, first landing and a long gallery.

The building was bequeathed in 1938 to the Society of the Cincinnati for its headquarters. This patriotic society has membership limited to first-born sons descended from officers in the Revolutionary Army or Navy or French allied forces who fought with them. Anderson was a member for 43 years. A number of rooms are filled with swords, decorations, dueling pistols, portraits and other memorabilia from the Revolutionary War period.

Armed Forces Medical Museum

In the grounds of Walter Reed Army Medical Center, entrance at 6825 16th St. N.W. (Building 54 on Dahlia St.)

Tel: 576-2418 (recorded) or 576-2348 (further inquiries). **Open:** May 1–Oct. 31 Mon.–Fri. 9:30 a.m.–5 p.m. Sat. & Sun. noon–5 p.m. Nov. 1–Apr. 30 Mon.–Fri. 9:30 a.m.–4:30 p.m. Sat. & Sun. 11:30 a.m.–4:30 p.m. **Admission:** Free. **Tours:** By appointment. Bus numbers S2 & S3 from downtown Washington.

A word of caution: this museum is not for the squeamish or anyone likely to be fazed out by bottled, grotesquely deformed human babies and Siamese twins, some of whom were born alive.

However, there are some sensational exhibits of historic interest which make the trip—exactly four miles north of the White House—morbidly alluring.

Bone fragments from President Abraham Lincoln's skull are encased next to the lead ball fired into his head by the assassin, John Wilkes Booth.

A segment of the yellowish vertebral column of another assassinated President, James Garfield, is also on public view. The path of the bullet stymied doctors in those pre-X-Ray days in 1881 but it is clearly visible from this autopsy evidence.

Perhaps the most bizarre exhibit is General Daniel Sickles' right leg bone, amputated during the Civil War battle of Gettysburg when shattered by a 12 lb. Confederate cannon ball. Sickles sent the limb to the museum together with his compliments.

Remember Able, the Rhesus monkey shot 300 miles into space in the nose cone of a Jupiter rocket in 1959? His entire skeletal remains are preserved here.

Not to be missed is the shrunken human head from Ecuador. There is also an embalmed head of a 12-year-old girl and the mummified head of an Egyptian adult male.

Chilling reminders of the past include a skull fractured by an Indian tomahawk.

Arts & Industries Building

Jefferson Drive at 9th St. N.W.

Tel: 357-2700. **Open:** Daily except Christmas 10 a.m.–5:30 p.m. **Admission:** Free. Museum shop. **Metro station:** Smithsonian on Blue or Orange lines.

After you've looked around here you'll understand why the Smithsonian Institution came to be labeled *The Nation's Attic*. Back in 1876, when the Centennial Exhibition closed in Philadelphia, most of the States and foreign exhibitors found it cheaper to donate their displays to the Federal government rather than ship them home. Congress had little choice but to vote $250,000 for a building to house the gifts.

The result was the National Museum, now known as the Arts & Industries Building. It was completed in 1881, just in time to be the site for President James Garfield's inaugural ball.

Here time is frozen in the 19th century. The largest exhibit is a 34 ton wood-burning passenger train locomotive and tender. Everyday transport of those days is carefully preserved in the carriages, buggies, carryalls and covered wagon.

The Philadelphia firm of Snediker & Carr has working models of its ventillating system next to a sign proclaiming: "All places are free from flies where our rotating fans are used." Another large exhibit is a lighthouse lens with 400,000 candlepower.

There are totem poles, a Gatling battery gun, electro-plated tableware, pocket watches, false teeth, swords, chamber room furniture, ladies period shoes and dresses, and advertisements for Madame Griswold's supporting corsets.

Don't miss the silver filigree jewelry from Norway, the exquisite traveling and jewel cases by Hurt & Roskell of London, and "Mrs. Potts' gold handled, double painted smoothing and polishing irons."

B'nai B'rith Klutznick Museum

1640 Rhode Island Ave. N.W.

Tel: 857-6583. **Open:** Sun.–Fri. 10 a.m.–5 p.m. Closed Sat. & legal and Jewish holidays. **Admission:** Free. **Metro station:** Farragut North on Red Line.

This small museum is the envy of many a grander archive because it has the original signed letter in which George Washington expresses democratic beliefs in no uncertain terms.

The founding father addressed the letter to the Hebrew Congregation of Newport, Rhode Island, which he visited in August 1790. Washington, who was then President, wrote that the government of the United States *"gives to bigotry no sanction, to persecution no assistance."*

The museum has a number of reminders of modern persecution against Jews abroad. There is a yellow star made of cotton and printed with the word *Jude,* which the Nazis forced Jews to wear. Also on display is currency used in the notorious Czechoslovak concentration camp of Theresienstadt.

An Indian prayerbook is a rare sight, particularly the one here in which each page in Hebrew has a facing translation in Sanskrit.

The ancient coin collection dates from 2nd century B.C.E. to 4th century C.E.

Many of the exhibits are from the 17th century, including an illustrated book of daily blessings from Holland, steel circumcision knives from Italy, silver candlesticks from Poland, and vividly decorated Italian parchment Scrolls of Esther, read on the festival of Purim.

A number of 19th century Austrian clocks and watches have Hebrew letters where it is usual to have Roman numerals.

Daughters of The American Revolution Headquarters & Museum

1776 D. St. N.W.

Tel: 628-1776. **Open:** Mon.–Fri. 9 a.m.–4 p.m. Sun. 1–5 p.m. **Admission:** Free. Gift shop. **Metro station:** Farragut West on Blue or Orange lines.

This colossal, classical building opposite the Ellipse is the repository of such rare items as one of the two original surviving tea chests from the famous Boston Tea Party of 1773. The museum also displays White House china designed by First Lady Caroline Harrison, who was the DAR's first President General.

The greatest drawcard is the more than two dozen State rooms with period furnishings showing the regional development of member States over the centuries. In one room there is a gilt armchair from the French furniture collection which drew the wrath of Congress because of the great amount of money which President Monroe paid for it.

In another room is a picture of the *Battle of Bennington* in 1777, which Anna Mary Robertson "Grandma" Moses painted and donated to the DAR in 1953.

The DAR was founded in 1890 by direct lineal descendants of those who served in the cause of Independence and visitors are taken through the Genealogical Library—one of the finest in the country—where Alex Halley did some of his research for his epic novel, *Roots.*

This spacious former auditorium was the site of the very first Arms Limitation Talks, which opened in 1921. On the wall above the porthole portrait of George Washington by Rembrandt Peale, is the Society's insignia, fashioned from a British cannon captured at Saratoga in 1777.

Department of The Interior Museum

C St. between 18th & 19th Sts. N.W.

Tel: 343-2743 **Open:** Mon.-Fri. 8 a.m.-4 p.m. **Admission:** Free.
Metro station: Farragut West on Blue or Orange lines.

This modest museum, tucked inside the labyrinthine corridors of the Department of the Interior, is a hodgepodge of Indian arts and crafts, geological samples, and interesting artifacts from the national heritage.

There are Pueblo drums, Apache basketwork, Hopi decorated pottery, a splendidly feathered Yakima Chief's headdress, and Cheyenne arrows which a soldier plucked from dying buffaloes at Fort Sill Indian Territory (Oklahoma) in 1868.

In the sampling of early land bounties you'll see the original bounty land warrant of 160 acres issued to Ulysses S. Grant, later President of the U.S., for services rendered in the Mexican War.

Chastening exhibits, designed to spotlight endangered species, show leopard-skin-trimmed sandals, and handbags and shoes made from crocodile skins. These and similar items are now on the list of banned imports. Close by is a mounted Heath Hen, a bird which became extinct in 1932 through overhunting and destruction of its habitat for agricultural development.

The Bureau of Mines display has radioactive uranium minerals and other specimens used in weapons of modern warfare. A separate geological survey has mineral specimens including a chunk of uranium ore of the type used to fuel nuclear reactors.

Among the many dioramas, maps, photographs and illustrations is a graphics display showing how Landsat, an unmanned satellite, collects data on the earth's features and resources.

Dolls' House & Toy Museum

5236 44th St. N.W.

Tel: 244-0024. **Open:** Tues.–Sat. 10 a.m.–5 p.m. Sun. noon–5 p.m. **Admission:** Adults $2, children under 14 $1. Gift Shop. **Metro station:** Friendship Heights on Red line.

Put it down to nostalgia for the past if you will, but more adults than children keep visiting what must rank as one of the world's best collections of antique dolls' houses and toys.

Founded in 1975 by dolls' house historian, Flora Gill Jacobs, the collection is so vast that only a fraction can be shown at any given time. Special displays are arranged at Easter, Halloween, Christmas and on other annual festive occasions.

While most of the dolls' houses, toys and games date back to the Victorian era, the entire collection falls into the antique classification.

The dolls' houses are faithful miniature reproductions of the architecture of yesteryear, as in the turn-of-the-century quintet of Baltimore row houses or the 18th century German kitchen.

Toys are made of wood, lithographed paper-on-wood and tin. Some of the delicate dinner and tea sets are fashioned from porcelain, pewter and glass. There are also Model T Fords, old trolleys and even Teddy Roosevelt on safari.

The miniature zoos, arks and games of a zoological nature were borrowed in their entirety for a special exhibition arranged by the Smithsonian Institution one winter at the National Zoological Park.

Also on show are card and board games about U.S. Presidents. They were manufactured by Parker Bros. at the turn of the century.

Dumbarton Oaks

1703 32nd St. N.W.

Tel: 338-8278 (recorded) and 342-3200 (further information).
Open: Collections, Tues.-Sun. 2-5 p.m., Gardens, daily except
holidays, 2-5 p.m. **Admission:** Free, gardens only $1. Gift shop.
No close Metro station—taxi recommended.

This palatial home on 16 acres of land hosted big-
power talks in 1944 to lay foundations for creation of
the United Nations.

It also gave its name, *Dumbarton Oaks Concerto,*
to composer Igor Stravinsky's *Concerto in E Flat*
because it was first performed in the renaissance music
room, here in the home of Mr. & Mrs. Robert Woods
Bliss, who commissioned the work.

The original home, since enlarged, was built in
1801 and named by its owner after the Rock of Dumbarton in Scotland. Mildred and Robert Bliss remodeled
it after taking possession in 1920.

In 1940 they gave it to Harvard University for use
as a research center in Byzantine and early Christian
studies.

Robert Bliss, former U.S. Ambassador to
Sweden and the Argentine, and his wife, heiress to a
fortune from children's medicine, built up the extensive collection of pre-Columbian, Byzantine and
Hellenistic art, jewelry and archaeological relics.

Their ashes are buried in the rose garden, part of
10 acres of formal gardens, with pools, terraces,
decorative sculptural work and paths.

The flora includes jasmine, crocus, honeysuckle,
evergreens, magnolias and Japanese cherry trees.

The pavilion built especially to house the ancient
artifacts was designed by Phillip Johnson.

Mrs. Bliss collaborated with landscape designer,
Beatrix Farrand on planning the extensive gardens,
which are nationally renowned.

Goddard Space Flight Center

Greenbelt, Md., 14 miles northeast of downtown Washington, off Baltimore-Washington Parkway, east of Beltway.

Tel: (301) 344-8103. **Open:** Wed.-Sun. 10 a.m.-4 p.m. Closed Thanksgiving, Christmas, New Year's Day. **Admission:** Free. Gift shop. No close Metro station. Private transport necessary.

The Visitor Center at this sprawling 1108 acres of one of NASA's largest research and development facilities is crammed with historic rockets, spacecraft, satellites and audio-visual information for the enjoyment of all ages.

One of the prized displays is the authentic Gemini XII spacecraft in which two astronauts sat cramped together for 59 earth orbits in 1966. The heat shield protecting Gemini spacecraft during re-entry stands nearby.

The space-tracking center where more than 2000 top scientists and engineers work, is named after the Massachusetts-born space flight pioneer, Dr. Robert Goddard, and a replica of the world's first liquid-fueled rocket he launched in 1926 is on view. His rocket shot 41 ft. high in 2½ seconds at a speed of 60 m.p.h. Model rockets are launched here on the first and third Sundays of the month, 1-2 p.m.

A collection of rockets on the terrace includes the sleek Iris, used mainly for flight tests in the early sixties, and the Javelin, which boosted the radio astronomy program.

Goddard's technicians, who track and communicate with orbiting satellites, relay the data to space scientists around the world. Visitors can listen in to recordings from space centers scattered around the U.S. and follow the weather situation on a computer color screen.

Jewish War Veterans National Museum

1811 R St. N.W.

Tel: 265-6280. **Open:** Mon.-Fri. 10 a.m.–4 p.m. Closed official and Jewish holidays. Sun. tours by pre-arrangement.**Admission:** Free. **Metro Station:** Dupont Circle on Red line.

The oldest active veterans organization in the U.S. moved into this Georgian building in 1984 and has since been expanding its museum by drawing on the more than one million items in its archives.

Here are the handwritten minutes of the 1896 meeting of Jewish Civil War veterans who decided to associate in response to a libelous article in the *Naval Review* magazine, stating that no Jews had served in either of the Civil War armies.

Pictorial displays cover Jewish participation in all U.S. wars, from the Revolutionary period through the Vietnam conflict.

Many Jews were awarded the Medal of Honor, the nation's highest decoration for valor, beginning with Sgt. Leopold Karpeles in the Civil War and more recently with 1st lieutenant Jack Jacobs in Vietnam. On view is the Medal of honor awarded during World War I to Sgt. Ben Kaufman, later JWV National Commander.

A more recent addition is a gold Mezzuzah found on the Chicamauga, Va. Civil War battlefield.

Preserved for posterity is a portable Ark crafted in the Solomon Islands in 1944 and used throughout the Pacific theater during World War II.

Six volumes of xeroxed copies of Adolf Eichmann's pre-trial testimony in German were donated by the Israel Police. Original printed items include battle plans for the invasion of Okinawa in 1945.

A 6 ft. high, 500-year-old hand-made brass Menorah, looted by the Nazis in Hungary and found by the allies in a cave in Germany, is another showpiece.

Lilian & Albert Small Jewish Museum of Washington

Corner of 3rd & G Sts. N.W.

Tel: 881-0100. **Open:** Sun. 11 a.m.–3 p.m. Mon.–Fri. by appointment. **Admission:** Free. **Metro station:** Judiciary Square on Red line (F St. exit).

President Ulysses S. Grant attended the dedication in 1876 of this first synagogue erected in the capital by orthodox members of Adas Israel congregation. It is the only synagogue, apart from the Touro in Newport, R.I., to be listed on the National Register of Historical Places.

However, it has been at its present location only since 1969. On a December day that year the entire 270-ton brick and wood structure was moved in a 2½ hour feat from three blocks away, to make room for the new Metro headquarters building.

In 1908 the large congregation moved to a new building while this structure was used as a Greek Orthodox Church and then even as the Dixie Pig Carry-Out Shops.

Now named for the Washington couple who financed much of the move and restoration, the synagogue is notable for its striking elegance and simplicity, the twin women's galleries, and the original Ark. During restoration, one of the original pews was brought back from southern Maryland after its discovery in a country church.

The street level floor, where the ritual bath and classrooms were located, now houses the small museum. There are changing exhibits but the permanent collection has a book in Hebrew, written to sound the phonetics of English; the original shovel used at ground-breaking ceremonies in 1876; and works by Phillip Ratner, best known for his sculptures at Ellis Island, New York.

Marine Corps Museum

Building 58, Charles Morris Ave., Washington Navy Yard, 9th & M Streets S.E.

Tel: 433-3840. **Open:** Mon.–Sat. 10 a.m.–4 p.m. Fri. in summer 6–8 p.m. Sun. noon-5 p.m. **Admission:** Free. Gift Shop. **Metro station:** Eastern market on Blue or Orange lines.

This is the home of the most famous U.S. flag of World War II. It was raised by marines atop Mt. Suribachi, Iwo Jima, after one of the bloodiest battles of the war, in which more than 5,000 marines were killed. The Pulitzer Prizewinning photograph of the flag-raising, snapped by Associated Press photographer Joe Rosenthal on 23 February 1945, was reproduced as the world's largest cast bronze statue and can be seen near Arlington national Cemetery (see page 98).

Many of the exhibits highlight the Marine Corps' role in the Pacific War from 1941 through 1945 and commemorate the island campaigns in which the marines were so conspicuously brave.

On view are captured Japanese Samurai swords, flags, weapons, and even eyeglasses, boots, currency and handwritten postcards. There are many cuttings and reproductions of contemporary U.S. newspapers and cartoons. The front page of the *Los Angeles Examiner* of 15 August 1945 screamed: WAR ENDS!

Another section has display cases with period uniforms and weapons from the inception of the Marine Corps. There is a cartridge pouch and money for monthly pay from the Revolutionary War. Though rusty-colored, the grape shot and chain shot—used to bring down masts—are in good condition.

Salvaged from the 1977 sale of the former Presidential yacht, *Sequoia,* is the log desk, upon which rests a visitors book for your signature and comments.

National Air & Space Museum

Independence Ave. at 6th St. S.W.

Tel: 357-2700. **Open:** Daily except Christmas 10 a.m.-5:30 p.m. **Admission:** Free. Gift shop and cafeteria. **Metro station:** Smithsonian or Blue or Orange lines.

The most popular of Washington's museums, and the most visited museum in the world, has 23 cavernous galleries devoted to the epic story of manned flight.

A star attraction is the plane flown by the pioneering Wright brothers at Kitty Hawk, North Carolina, in 1903. And dwarfed by the space-age rockets is the silver-colored *Spirit of St. Louis,* in which Charles Lindbergh flew the first solo, nonstop trans-Atlantic flight from New York to Paris in 1927. The museum also houses the original *Double Eagle II,* the gondola in which three men from Albuquerque, New Mexico, made the first crossing of the Atlantic by balloon in 1978.

A special gallery devoted to World War II aviation includes a Mitsubishi Zero Japanese naval fighter used in the attack on Pearl Harbor, and a British Spitfire.

Among the rockets and spacecraft, you can touch the Mercury Spacecraft *Friendship 7* in which John Glenn became the first American to orbit the earth in February 1962. Here, too, is *Columbia,* the Apollo 11 command module which brought back the first men on the moon on that memorable July 1969.

Video screens show movies of the space shuttle, pioneers of flight and Coast Guard rescue operations. A movie theater with a giant screen, shows films on flight and the living planet.

National Archives

Constitution Avenue between 7th & 9th Sts. N.W.

Tel: 523-3184. **Open:** Daily 10 a.m.-5:30 p.m. Apr.-Labor Day to 9 p.m. **Admission:** Free. Gift shop. **Metro station:** Archives on Yellow line or Smithsonian on Blue or Orange lines.

At 10 a.m. daily, two bronze doors, each almost 39 ft. high, 10 ft. wide and 11 in. thick, slide open at the National Archives to admit the public to view the most precious documents in the United States.

Protected by helium and water vapor within glass and bronze cases are the original Declaration of Independence, the Constitution and the Bill of Rights. At night, and during emergencies, these irreplacable treasures are lowered electrically 20 ft., into a 50-ton vault for safekeeping.

The Declaration of Independence, drafted during a 17-day period by Thomas Jefferson and four colleagues, was adopted by the Continental Congress on July 4, 1776.

Below it, on the left, are the first and signature pages of the four-sheet Constitution. It was signed by representatives of the founding states on September 17, 1787.

The single sheet of parchment next to this is the Bill of Rights. Though it contains 12 Articles, only the last 10 were ratified by three quarters of the founding states as amendments to the Constitution.

Other documents flank the Charters of Freedom in permanent display. Among these is the Treaty of Paris by which King George III of Great Britain recognized the Independence of the United States on September 3, 1783.

National Building Museum

Judiciary Square N.W., between 4th & 5th Sts. Entrance on F. St.

Tel: 272-2877. **Open:** Mon.-Fri. 10 a.m.-4 p.m. Sat.-Sun. noon-4 p.m. **Admission:** Free. **Metro station:** Judiciary Square on Red line (F St. exit).

The tallest Corinthian columns the world has ever seen tower inside this monstrously large former Pension Building. Each of the eight columns—bulging with a circumference of 25 ft.—soars 75 ft. high. This is 15 ft. higher than the tallest columns the Romans ever built, at a temple in Baalbek, Lebanon, in 1st century A.D.

Designed as a memorial to Civil War veterans, the building was completed in 1885 at a cost of $886,000. For the next 40 years it was used as the Pension Bureau and thereafter for various government agencies. On eight occasions it was the setting for sparkling Presidential inaugural balls.

The architect, General Montgomery Meigs, based his design on the renaissance Palazzo Farnese in Rome. Measuring 400 ft. by 200 ft. and 159 ft. high, it was the largest brick building in the world when completed. But not everyone admired it. General Tecumseh Sherman snorted: "The worst of it is, it is fireproof!"

The 1200 ft. long, and 3 ft. high frieze around the building, between the first and second floors, is the largest example of sculptured terra cotta work in the U.S. Designed by Caspar Buberl, the 1355 figures in the procession represent units of the Union Army.

Visitors will also see the original plans for Washington, D.C. and for major U.S. monuments, in rooms set aside for exhibitions.

National Firearms Museum

1600 Rhode Island Ave. N.W.

Tel. 828-6198. **Open:** Daily 10 a.m.-4 p.m. **Admission:** Free. **Metro station:** Dupont Circle on Red line or Farragut West on Blue or Orange lines.

Hundreds of weapons tracing the history of firearms are neatly labeled with brief explanatory notes inside the headquarters building of the National Rifle Association.

On show is one of the more than 100,000 muzzle-loading muskets bought by the U.S. from France during the Revolutionary War.

Here, too, is the ivory-handled .45 calibre Colt revolver which belonged to Erle Stanley Gardner, creator of defense attorney, Perry Mason.

Some of the weapons are used to illustrate the art of gunmaking and milestones in handgun and rifle development. Among the earliest firearms is a 40 oz. German muzzle-loading pistol made about 400 years ago. A muzzle-loading gun manufactured in India is 69.8 inches long.

This is the permanent home of a flintlock rifle, similar to those used by the earliest colonists, which the gunsmith and General Staff of the Texas Army—inspired by President Reagan's courage—presented to him after he was wounded in the assassination attempt.

Among the air guns, shot guns, heavy game rifles, and pistols, are weapons of the type used by the U.S. team at the Los Angeles Olympics of 1984.

The collection of Russian military rifles includes the semi-automatic Tokarev rifle used so widely in World War II. Other exhibits include an Austrian crossbow made about 1565, a 17th century Japanese Samurai short sword, hunting knives and a 19th century barrel rifling machine.

National Museum of American History

Madison Drive between 12th & 14th Sts. N.W.

Tel: 357-2700. **Open:** Daily except Christmas 10 a.m.-5:30 p.m. **Admission:** Free. Gift shop & cafeteria. **Metro station:** Smithsonian or Federal Triangle on Blue or Orange lines.

Unique exhibits from instant and recent history make this one of the most exciting museums in the nation. Only here will you find a room full of original, formal gowns worn by the First Ladies from Martha Washington to Nancy Reagan. Here, too, is Alexander Graham Bell's first telephone, Thomas Edison's light bulb and millions of stamps making up the National Postage Stamp Collection.

Among other highlights in these three spacious floors is the gigantic and tattered Star Spangled Banner, which inspired Francis Scott Key to write the National Anthem as it flew over Fort McHenry, Baltimore, during an attack by the British fleet in 1814.

On the same ground floor are the ruby slippers worn by Judy Garland in the 1939 MGM film, *The Wizard of Oz.* They can be seen in the Nation of Nations display, together with Archie Bunker's chair and Muhammed Ali's boxing gloves.

At an exhibition titled *Campaigning American Style,* you can peek into the comfortable interior of President Kennedy's campaign jet, the *Caroline.*

There is a pen used by President Johnson when signing the bill establishing the Kennedy Center. Next to it is the original draft musical score of the *Mass,* composed by Leonard Bernstein for the opening of the Kennedy Center in 1971.

From the pioneer days of transport there's more than you bargained for, with vintage cars, bicycles and wagons.

National Museum of Natural History

Madison Drive & 10th St. N.W.

Tel: 357-2700. **Open:** Daily except Christmas 10 a.m.-5:30 p.m.
Tarantula feedings: Weekdays 10:30 a.m., 11:30 a.m., 1:30 p.m.
Weekends 11:30 a.m., 12:30 p.m., 1:30 p.m. **Admission:** Free. Gift
shop and cafeteria. **Metro station:** Smithsonian or Federal Triangle
on Blue or Orange lines.

A few hours at the very minimum should be given
to this enormous museum with rare and wondrous offerings for all ages.

Many visitors are mesmerized by the hairy black
and orange Tarantula spiders and black scorpions
among the live exhibits.

There are gasps of a different kind in the dazzling
Hall of Gems. Encased here is the 45.5 carat Hope
Diamond, whose last private owner was former
Washington Post owner, Evalyn Walsh McLean.

The range of exhibits runs the full spectrum from
the dawn of creation, with 360-million-year-old
fossilized lobe-finned fish, to pieces of moon rock.
The skeleton of a 90 ft. long Diplodocus—largest of
all the dinosaurs—dwarfs the 30 ft. long giant squid,
washed ashore on Plum Island, Mass. A stuffed 8-ton,
13 ft. high Angolan elephant reigns supreme under the
Rotunda while an 857 lbs. Bengal Tiger, believed to be
the largest ever slain in India, leaps out at entrants to
the gift shop.

Human exhibits include a supine Egyptian mummy and a Peruvian mummy preserved by dry desert
air. In a room devoted to Dynamics of Evolution
you'll see many bottled and preserved reptiles and
mammals.

Separate halls contain large presentations of
birds, sea life, fossils, items from Pacific, Indian,
Eskimo, Asian and African cultures, reptiles,
minerals, fossils, insects, and meteorites.

Navy Memorial Museum

Building 76, Washington Navy Yard, 9th & M Sts. S.E.

Tel: 433-2651. **Open:** Daily Sept.-May 9 a.m.-4 p.m., Sat.-Sun. 10 a.m.-5 p.m. June-Aug. 9 a.m.-5 p.m. Gift shop. **Metro station:** Eastern Market on Blue or Orange lines.

Outstanding among the unique collection are the metal replicas of the two atom bombs dropped over Japan in 1945. Also here is the guest book from *USS Augusta,* signed by President Truman and King George VI just before the President sailed across the Atlantic from Plymouth, England, that fateful August. Close by is the ship's bell from the German cruiser, *S.S. Prinz Eugen,* which surrendered to British forces in Copenhagen that year.

Of more recent vintage is the space suit worn by Capt. John Young, commander of the Apollo 16 manned lunar landing mission in 1972. Harrowing exhibits from the Vietnam War include the navy watch cap worn through almost nine winters by POW Lt. Everett Alvarez, the first U.S. Navy pilot captured.

A World War II F4U Corsair fighter plane is suspended from the ceiling. Down below in a glass case is the service dress blue blouse which belonged to the Commander in Chief of U.S. Naval Forces during World War II, Admiral Ernest King.

From further back in history are the program for the funeral procession of British Admiral Lord Nelson, relics from Admiral Farragut's flagship at New Orleans and Mobile Bay, and Commodore Stephen Decatur's certificate of membership in the Society of the Cincinnati, signed by George Washington. The original rigged foremast fighting top platform from the frigate, *Constitution,* the oldest commissioned ship in the U.S. Navy, is a specially prized exhibit.

Smithsonian Institution Building ("The Castle")

Jefferson Drive at 10th St. S.W.

Tel: 357-2700. **Open:** Daily except Christmas 10 a.m.-5:30 p.m. **Admission:** Free. **Metro station:** Smithsonian on Blue or Orange lines.

In a room to the left of the entrance lie the remains of James Smithson, the Englishman who bequeathed $500,000 to the U.S. for the founding in Washington, "under the name of the Smithsonian Institution, an establishment for the increase and diffusion of knowledge among men."

Smithson's tomb was brought from Genoa, Italy in 1904 when authorities there said they needed that cemeterial land for quarrying. Look closely and you'll see that the age of this "gentleman scientist", who was an expert on minerals, is incorrectly carved onto the tomb as 75. When he died in 1829, Smithson was only 64.

Smithson's bequest was shipped across the Atlantic Ocean as gold sovereigns in sacks filling 11 boxes. The interest financed this, the first of the Smithsonian buildings, which remains the administrative headquarters for the entire museum complex.

James Renwick, Jr. designed the red Seneca sandstone building in the Norman style of the 12th century. The structure was completed in 1855.

The Visitor Information and Associates Reception Center is in the Great Hall.

A permanent collection of drawings and models in the Great Hall shows plans for the development of Washington from its inception to those which have been drawn up for future expansion.

The "Castle" also houses the Woodrow Wilson International Center for Scholars, which Congress established as the official "living memorial" to him.

Textile Museum

2320 S Street, N.W.

Tel: 667-0441 **Open:** Tues.-Sat. 10 a.m.-5 p.m. Sun. 1-5 p.m. Closed Mon. & public holidays **Library:** Wed.-Fri. 10 a.m.-5 p.m. Sat. 10 a.m.-1 p.m. **Admission:** Free, but suggested donations of $2 adults, 50¢ children. **Tours:** Sat. 1-3 p.m. Group tours require 3 weeks advance notice.

This amazing collection of more than 10,000 textiles and 1,100 carpets from the suqs of the Middle East to the countryside of Peru began in 1898 when the founder, George Hewitt Myers (1875-1957) bought an oriental rug for his dormitory at Yale University.

It remains the only museum in the Western hemisphere devoted solely to the collection, study, preservation and display of historic and handmade textiles and carpets.

Myers amassed so many priceless items that only a minute fraction can be exhibited at any one time. They are shown in galleries inside a former townhouse, which Myers bought adjacent to his own home. The stately houses are connected by an indoor passageway.

Myers' gracious residence was built in 1916 by the celebrated architect, John Russell Pope, who also designed the Jefferson Memorial, the National Archives, the West Wing of the National Gallery of Art and the Brazilian Embassy. The former library room is now an exotic museum shop. Another spacious wood-paneled room serves as a shop gallery for the sale of works by contemporary fiber artists and crafts people.

If your visit coincides with the first Saturday in June you're in for a lot of fun at the annual *Celebration of Textiles Day,* when live sheep are sometimes sheared and other hands-on activities scheduled.

LANDMARK
BUILDINGS

The Supreme Court

Bureau of Engraving and Printing

14th & C Sts. S.W.

Tel: 447-9709. **Open:** Mon.–Fri. 8 a.m.–2 p.m. **Admission:** Free.
Gift Shop. **Metro station:** Smithsonian on Blue or Orange Lines.

This is the closest you'll ever get to billions of dollars because here's where they print the greenbacks. There are stacks of them—sometimes in piles $32 million high.

The only thing between them and your claws are shatter-proof glass windows and one of the tightest security systems in the country. Photography is forbidden.

The free tour along a fixed route takes about 45 minutes. When you get to the end you can buy a package of $150 just by dropping 50 cents into a vending machine. The catch is that all the money's shredded because these sheets of bills didn't pass the printing inspection test and the guys at the top figured they could still make money on defects.

As the principal product of the Bureau is U.S. paper currency, this is all you'll see inside the plant. All told, about $20 billion is printed here every year. This mostly replaces worn or mutilated bills, regularly taken out of circulation because the average life of a dollar bill is only 18 months.

During the tour you'll see high speed Rotary presses churning out more than 7000 sheets of bills every hour.

As the sign says: "The Buck Starts Here!"

The final stop is above two-color presses, over-printing with green ink for the serial numbers and the U.S. Treasury seal, and with black ink for numerals and the Federal Reserve district seal.

The bills are then banded into packages for shipment to an eager market.

Capitol

Capitol Hill, between Constitution Ave. & Independence Ave.

Tel: Guide Service 225-6827. **Open:** Free tours daily every 15 minutes, 9 a.m.–3:45 p.m. **Admission:** Free. Gift shop & cafeteria. **Metro station:** Capitol South on Blue or Orange lines.

The domed white Capitol is the symbol of the nation's democracy where elected Senators and Representatives meet in separate wings to make the laws. It is built on a hill which the 18th century planner, Pierre L'Enfant, described as "a pedestal waiting for a monument."

George Washington laid the cornerstone on September 18, 1793. Since then the building has been enlarged, altered and even rebuilt after British soldiers burned the interior in 1814.

Begin your sightseeing in the *Rotunda* where you can join a free half hour tour. The Rotunda is 180 feet high and 97 feet across. It is crowned by a nine million pound cast-iron dome completed in 1865. Much of the art work here is by Constantino Brumidi, an immigrant artist who fled his native Italy as a political refugee in 1852.

To get to *Statuary Hall* go through the door between the statues of Jefferson and Washington. This hall was the House of Representatives until 1857 when the legislators moved to their present quarters. The acoustics here are notoriously bad. Stand above the small bronze disk on the floor and you will hear clearly what is whispered from 45 feet away. The disk marks the spot where John Quincy Adams had his desk as a Representative after serving as sixth President of the United States.

The *House of Representatives* is the largest legislative chamber in the world. The Speaker of the House sits behind the walnut desk on the uppermost rostrum. Whenever the President addresses a joint ses-

63

The Capitol

sion of Congress he stands on the dias immediately below the Speaker. Members of the majority party sit on the Speaker's right and the minority party on his left.

The *Senate* has occupied its dignified chamber since 1859. Each of the 100 Senators has an allotted desk. By tradition, Senators with seniority sit in the front rows. The Vice President of the United States, who presides over the Senate, sits the rostrum in front of the national flag and below the press gallery.

In the *Crypt* you'll see the former Supreme Court chamber. One level below is the black-shrouded bier on which many presidents lay in state in the Rotunda before burial.

Christian Heurich Mansion

1307 New Hampshire Ave., N.W. between 19th & 20th Sts.

Tel: 785-2068. Open: Wed., Fri. Sat. noon–4 p.m. Victorian garden open Mon.–Fri. 10:30 a.m.–5 p.m. **Admission:** (to mansion) $2 includes half-hour guided tour. Gift shop & cafeteria. **Metro station:** Dupont Circle on Red line.

Brewing magnate Christian Heurich built this baronial downtown mansion in 1892–4 and lived in it until he died aged 102 in 1945. Even his mausoleum in Rock Creek Cemetery, with a stained glass window by Tiffany of New York, singled him out as extraordinary.

Heurich left school in his native Germany aged 14 and was apprenticed as a butcher and brewer before immigrating when 23-years-old. In 1872 he leased a local brewery, married the landlord's widow the following year, and inherited the brewery on her death six years later.

This opulent landmark was given to the Columbia Historical Society by Heurich's third wife shortly before her death in 1956. The mansion, furnished and fitted in the feudal style of the late 19th century, was built with poured concrete, making it the capital's first fire-proof residence.

Many of the 31 rooms have splendidly decorated ceilings and carved Spanish mahogany paneling. There are 17 fireplaces, stenciled wall surfaces and a grand staircase of marble and onyx.

A gilded Steinway grand piano stands below a wood-carved musicians' gallery in the music room. Access to the dining room is through one of the many 15 ft. high doorways. The oak-carved extension table seats 16.

The Victorian garden is popular with office workers during lunch breaks. Many buy their meals in the restaurant in the old carriage house, where food is sold only for take-out.

Clara Barton Home

5801 Oxford Rd., Glen Echo, Md. About 7 miles northwest of downtown Washington, D.C.

Tel: 492-6245. Open: Daily 10 a.m.–5 p.m. **Admission:** Free. 20 min. guided tours. **Metro station:** Friendship Heights on Red line, then 20 minute ride over 4 miles on N5 or N8 bus, followed by a 200 yard walk.

Clara Barton, founder and first President of the American Red Cross, lived in this 35-room house for the last 15 years of her life. It was also the relief agency's administrative headquarters and warehouse for supplies.

The hemlock planks used in the steamboat Gothic design and railed galleries were taken from the dismantled Red Cross hotel in Johnstown, Pa., after Clara Barton had gone to the assistance of victims of the flood of 1889.

Her friend, Dr. Julian Hubbell, the first field agent for the American Red Cross, designed the four-story house. It was completed in 1891.

Though much of the furniture is from the same period, originals which belonged to the nonagerian at her death in 1912 include her work desk and the square grand piano made by Emerson Piano Company of Boston.

There are several old Royal typewriters, an antique telephone, a gramophone which had to be wound up, portable bath tubs in the bedrooms, and a coal-burning stove in the central hallway.

The walls are hung with many photographs of Clara Barton, the first woman to hold a government appointment—in the Patent Office.

She began her relief work on the Civil War battlefields and successfully lobbied Congress to ratify the Treaty of Geneva, thereby establishing the American Red Cross in 1882.

Decatur House

748 Jackson Place N.W.

Tel: 673-4030. **Open:** Feb.–Dec. Tues.–Fri. 10 a.m.–2 p.m. Sat. & Sun. noon–4 p.m. **Admission:** Adults $2.50, Children $1.25. Gift shop. **Metro station:** Farragut West on Blue or Orange lines.

This first private home on Lafayette Square was built in 1819 by naval hero Commodore Stephen Decatur, best known for the abridged version of his banquet toast: "Our country—right or wrong!"

Decatur and his wife, Susan, lived in it only 14 months before he died in the house from wounds sustained in a duel—only two days after he hosted a wedding ball for the daughter of President James Monroe.

Decatur paid for the elegant four-story brick Federal town house with prize money from victories over the Barbary pirates. The designer, Benjamin Latobe, was an English immigrant who became "the father of American architecture."

A succession of later occupants included French, British and Russian diplomats, Henry Clay, Martin Van Buren, Vice President George Dallas and other luminaries who presided over glittering social gatherings.

The home was given to the National Trust for Historic Preservation by the last owner, Marie Oge Beale, who had the house restored to the original plan in 1944. The second floor has the original Victorian furnishings from the two generations of Beale family occupants.

The first floor has a magnificent French four-poster bed owned by Stephen Decatur's father. One of Decatur's silver and ivory swords presented for heroism in the War of 1812 is on display.

The street level shop is noted for the originality and good taste of its gift and souvenir items.

Explorers' Hall

Corner of M & 17th Sts. N.W.

Tel: 857-7588. **Open:** Mon.–Sat. 9 a.m.–5 p.m. Sun. 10 a.m.–5 p.m. **Admission:** Free. Gift shop. **Metro station:** Farragut North or Dupont Circle on Red line.

Here in the *National Geographic Society's* downtown exhibition hall, you can join deep-sea divers plucking a 17th century bronze cannon from a sunken Spanish galleon on the floor of the sea off Florida. As color film of the adventure rolls on a video screen, you can rest assured it's for real by reaching out and touching the salvaged rusty cannon right next to you.

This is one of hundreds of exhibits guaranteed to bring home the thrill of adventure and discovery in the oceans and jungles of our planet.

Also here is the Sea Sled which underwater explorer Jacques Cousteau used to film five miles down in the mid-Atlantic Ocean.

On view is one of the sledges dragged by Huskies when Admiral Robert Peary became the first man to reach the North Pole. You'll see the frail U.S. flag that accompanied him, and listen to his recorded voice.

Did you know there are giant frogs in West Africa, fully 2 ft. long and weighing 7 lbs! Believe it or not, you'll see one preserved right here.

Among the permanent exhibits is the world's largest unmounted globe, made of aluminum and fiberglass, weighing more than 1000 lbs. and measuring 11 ft. between the North and South Poles.

A gargantuan head from the tropical wilds of Tabasco, Mexico, sits on the floor just as it was found by an expedition in 1939. Only this is a full-size cast of one of the 11 basalt Olmec heads.

FBI Headquarters

Pennsylvania Ave. between 9th & 10th Sts. N.W.

Tel: 324-3447. **Open:** Mon.–Fri. 9 a.m.–4:15 p.m. **Admission:** Free.
Metro station: Federal Triangle on Blue or Orange lines, or Archives
on Yellow line.

The famed federal agents who track down spies,
gangsters and criminals across the United States offer
free 75 minute guided tours for a peek into their
fortress-like headquarters in downtown Washington.

The tour takes you past photographs of Chicago
gangster Al Capone and other mobsters, gunmen and
robbers. There are also mug shots of the Ten Most
Wanted Fugitives.

One exhibit includes wreckage from a plane crash
and a photograph of the man hunted down by the
Feds, and subsequently executed, for placing a bomb
in his mother's suitcase so he could claim insurance
money on her life.

A special area honors J. Edgar Hoover, the legendary director of the FBI from 1924 until his death in
1972. On display is the simple office desk from which
the nation's top crime-buster issued directives to
agents across the land.

The FBI uses computers to keep on top of more
sophisticated crime. More than 25,000 fingerprints
received daily are processed by a computer called "the
finder".

Visitors are seated behind the bullet-proof glass
for a demonstration by special agents at target practice
in the indoor firearms range.

Dedicated in 1975, the building is the costliest
ever raised by the Public Buildings Service. It is also
one of the most controversial, having drawn few
defenders in the unrelenting criticism of its ugliness.

Folger Shakespeare Library

201 East Capitol St. S.E.

Tel: 544-7077. **Open:** Daily, Apr. 15–Labor Day, 10 a.m.–4 p.m.
Rest of year Mon.–Sat. 10 a.m.–4 p.m. **Admission:** Free. Gift shop.
Metro station: Capitol South on Blue or Orange Lines.

Only a block behind the Capitol, this building enfolds a vision of Shakespeare's age like a time capsule. There is a wooden three-tiered Elizabethan innyard theatre. As wondrous is the oak-paneled Great Hall, strung with majestic-looking 16th century English heraldic flags.

To top it all there's a sense of being amongst the world's largest collection of Shakespeare's printed works and in the repository of more than half of all books published in English before 1641. All told, there are more than 260,000 books and manuscripts, of which 100,000 are rare.

All this was the gift of a former Chairman of Standard Oil of New York, Henry Clay Folger, and his wife, Emily.

Folger's life-long romance with Shakespeareana began at Amherst College where he attended a lecture on the Bard by Ralph Waldo Emerson. Folger died in 1930—only two weeks after laying the cornerstone of this building.

Notable among the portraits lining the Great Hall is one of England's famed Shakespearean actor, David Garrick, painted in the 18th century by Sir Joshua Reynolds.

Also here is Garrick's massive chair, on which his head is carved in relief, supposedly by William Hogarth.

The Anne Hathaway Art Gallery is the venue for changing exhibitions of arts and crafts. Plays by Shakespeare and more modern playwrights are regularly staged in the Folger Theatre.

Ford's Theater & Lincoln Museum

511 10th St., N.W.

Tel: 426-6924. **Open:** Daily 9 a.m.–5 p.m. Thurs. to noon, Sat. & Sun. to 1 p.m. **Admission:** Free. Book shop. **Metro station:** Metro Center on Red, Blue or Orange lines.

The red-brick theater where an assassin shot President Lincoln at point-blank range has been restored almost exactly as it was on that fateful Good Friday, April 14, 1865. Visitors usually spend much longer in the basement-level Lincoln Museum where exhibits include the assassin's pistol and the clothes worn by Lincoln at the evening performance.

Lincoln sat in a rocking chair in the flag-draped presidential box, watching the comedy *Our American Cousin*. The killer, John Wilkes Booth, made his way through the lobby, up the winding staircase and along a narrow passageway to the unguarded door of the chief executive's box.

At 10:15 p.m. he leveled his Derringer and shot the President behind the left ear. Major Henry Rathbone, who together with his fiancée and Mrs. Lincoln were the only others in the box, struggled briefly with Booth.

As the assassin leapt onto the stage he caught his spur on the Treasury Guard's flag hanging from the presidential box and fractured his left leg.

In the pandemonium, Booth escaped into the back alley, mounted his horse and galloped away. Federal cavalrymen cornered and slew him 12 days later on a farm in Virginia.

Across the road is *Petersen House*. Physicians laid the 6 ft. 4 in. unconscious President diagonally across the small bed.

At 7:22 the following morning Abraham Lincoln died as rain fell outside.

Frederick Douglass Home

1411 W. St. S.E.

Tel: 426-5960/3. **Open:** Daily Apr.–Sept. 9 a.m.–5 p.m., Oct.–Mar. 9 a.m.–4 p.m. **Admission:** Free. Half-hour movie at Visitor Information Center, free, every hour 9 a.m.–3 p.m. Gift shop. No close Metro station. On Gray Line & Tourmobile routes.

This 21-room house of a famous fugitive slave turned abolitionist leader, Frederick Douglass, is the first official U.S. historic site honoring a black person. It is administered by the National Park Service which provides the guides.

Built in 1855 and purchased by Douglass in 1877 for $6,700, it was his home until his death in 1895.

The wood-framed 3-story home, on the crown of a hill in Washington's southeastern Anacostia district, provides a sweeping view of the capital and its most noted landmarks—the Washington Monument and the Capitol.

Almost all the fixtures and furnishings are originals. In the Visitor Information Center at the base of the hill is a death mask of the famed author and orator, and a copy of the *North Star* weekly newspaper he edited in 1849.

Other mementoes cover the period when he was U.S. Marshal of the District of Columbia, Recorder of Deeds in the capital, then U.S. Minister to Haiti.

The life-size sculpture is the work of Ed Dwight, who also created the bust of Martin Luther King, Jr. in Atlanta, Ga.

On view is the book-lined library with his work desk, Victorian washing utensils in the bedrooms, silverware in the dining room and the kitchen, and a wall calendar dated 1885. Also displayed are his carved walking sticks and his thin-framed spectacles.

Islamic Center

2551 Massachusetts Ave. N.W.

Tel: 332-8343. **Open:** Guided tours Sun.-Thurs. 10 a.m.–5 p.m.
Fri. 2-5 p.m. **Admission:** Free. Gift shop. No close Metro.

While people of all faiths are welcome, visitors must conform to dress requirements. Women must cover their heads, arms and legs and everyone must remove their shoes before entering the mosque.

The focal point of the buildings on this 30,000 sq. ft. of prime property along Embassy Row is the exquisitely-decorated mosque, built at an angle of about 60 degrees from Massachusetts Avenue so that it faces the holy city of Mecca in Saudi Arabia.

The minaret soars 160 ft. above the layers of Persian carpets which were donated by Iran. During a two-year period when fanatics gained control of the mosque in the early eighties, they tried to erase the name of the Shah of Iran, woven into a central carpet. The blue scratch marks are still visible.

The extremists burned the Egyptian pulpit, inlaid with ivory and ebony. It has been replaced by a wooden one provided by Syria.

The decorated porcelain wall tiles were made in Turkey while the great chandeliers were gifts from Egypt. A marble table, decorated with floral designs, was given by Afghanistan.

The need for a Center was decided on shortly after World War II by Washington-based diplomats from Islamic countries. Plans, supervised by the Egyptian Ministry of Wakfs, were designed by Mario Roosi, an Italian architect of several mosques, and a convert to Islam.

The Center includes cloisters, a library, classrooms, and an auditorium in the basement of the mosque.

Kennedy Center

2700 F St. N.W.

Tel: 254-3600 (information) and 857-0900 (charge tickets). **Open:** Daily 10 a.m.–end of eve. shows. **Admission:** Free. Free 40 minute tours, every 15 mins., daily 10 a.m.–1 p.m. Gift shop and cafeteria. **Metro station:** Foggy Bottom on Blue or Orange Lines then long 3-block walk. On Gray Line & Tourmobile routes.

The hub of Washington's cultural life is this plushly decorated center for the performing arts on the east bank of the Potomac River. Blocks of white marble from the Carrara quarries in Italy enclose the Opera House, Concert Hall, Eisenhower Theater and the American Film Institute Theater. From the roof terrace with restaurants there is a superb view of the capital and the Virginia shoreline across the river.

The Kennedy Center's three theaters are on the plaza level. Largest among them is the Concert Hall. Decorated in gold and white, it has a seating capacity of 2750. Norway presented the shimmering crystal chandeliers. Almost as large is the 2300 seat Opera House, where ballet performances and musical theater are staged. The red and gold silk stage curtain was a gift from Japan and the great chandelier from Austria.

The Eisenhower Theater presents the best of American and international plays in a 1200 seat auditorium. Canada donated the red and black stage curtain.

Also on the main floor is the American Film Institute Theater which regularly screens rare classic and foreign films.

One of the biggest draws is the massive bronze bust of the slain president, sculpted by the American, Robert Berks. It is displayed in the 630-feet-long Grand Foyer, majestically adorned with a gift of mirrors from Belgium and 18 sparkling chandeliers given by Sweden.

Library of Congress

1st St. at Independence Ave. S.E.

Tel: 287-5458. **Open:** Tours every hour on the hour, preceded by 15 min. slide show before every hour. Mon.–Fri. 9 a.m.–4 p.m. **Admission:** Free. Gift shop. **Metro station:** Capitol South on Blue or Orange lines.

The world's largest library stuffs 76 million items into 350 miles of bookshelves in three gigantic buildings on Capitol Hill. It also houses the papers of 23 U.S. Presidents from Washington to Coolidge. Here is the world's largest collection of cartographic materials and foreign, international and comparative law books. There are 10 million prints and photographs, 6 million pieces of music, autographed scores and composers' and musicians' correspondence, 500,000 sound recordings and more than 3 million microfilms.

Begun in 1800 with a $5000 grant from Congress, the Library was burned by the British in 1814 then begun anew with the acceptance of an offer by Thomas Jefferson of his collection of 6487 books.

The ornate *Thomas Jefferson Building,* completed in 1897, is the showpiece building, next to the Supreme Court. A visitors' gallery overlooks the octagonal Main Reading Room with its mahogany desks. The uppermost part of the dome is 160 ft. high.

Directly across Independence Avenue is the *James Madison Building,* opened in 1980. It encloses an area greater than 35 football fields. This is the location of the copyright office, geography room, law library, presidential papers, prints & photographs, motion picture and television reading rooms. Some of these originals are displayed in changing exhibitions.

Diagonally opposite is the *John Adams Building,* opened in 1939. It has African, Asian, Hebraic, Near East, Science and Social Science reading rooms.

Mount Vernon

16 miles south of downtown Washington, along Mt. Vernon Memorial Highway, Va.

Tel: (703) 780-2000. **Open:** Daily 9 a.m.–5 p.m., Nov. thru Feb. to 4 p.m. **Admission:** Adults $4, Children 6–11 $2. Gift shop and cafeteria. No close Metro station. On Gray Line and Tourmobile routes.

The country estate where George Washington lived and died is set atop a Virginia hill overlooking the Potomac River and Maryland. It is 16 miles south of downtown Washington, D.C.

During the Revolutionary War a British warship anchored nearby and the sailors invaded Mt. Vernon, abducting 20 servants and carrying off provisions. When he learned of the raid, Washington wrote angrily to his estate manager: "It would have been less painful to have heard that in consequence of your non-compliance with their request, they had burnt my house and laid the plantation in ruins. You ought to have considered yourself as my representative, and should have reflected on the bad example of communicating with the enemy."

Visitors approach the mansion around the grand sweep of grass past *slave quarters*. The adjacent museum is filled with personal clothing, jewelry and other possessions of George and Martha Washington.

The tour of the mansion begins in the *Banqueting Hall* where Washington hosted a stream of notables. The columned *verandah* facing the Potomac River was built in 1777 with floor stones from England.

Hanging on the wall in the *Central Hall* is the key to the Bastille prison of 18th century Paris. It was a gift to Washington from the Marquis de Lafayette. Opposite is the *Little Parlor* with an English harpsichord.

Next to this room is the *West Parlor*. As in other homes in colonial Virginia, Washington's mansion

Mount Vernon

had a downstairs bedroom. The *family dining room* is by the staircase.

George and Martha Washington's bedroom is at the end of the passage upstairs. It contains the bed on which the 6 ft. 2 in. first chief executive died on December 14, 1799 at the age of 67.

The downstairs *library* is where Washington came immediately after waking up. His dressing table can be seen below the window.

On your way down to the Washington tombs you pass by the *kitchen*. The downhill path forks right to the brick *tomb* with the marble sarcophagi of George and Martha Washington.

National Shrine of The Immaculate Conception

4th St. & Michigan Ave. N.E.

Tel: 526-8300. **Open:** Daily 7 a.m.–6 p.m. Guided tours from Visitor Center Mon.–Sat. 9 a.m.–4 p.m. Sun. 1:30–4 p.m. **Admission:** Free. Gift shop & cafeteria. **Metro station:** Brookland-CUA on Red line.

The building statistics make this the seventh largest church in the world and the biggest Catholic church in the U.S.A.

The great dome is 108 ft. in diameter and 237 ft. from the floor to the top of the cross. Built of stone, brick, tile and concrete in the shape of a Latin cross, this structure enfolds no less than 57 chapels and 3 oratories. The 329 ft. high Knights' Tower holds a 56 bell carillon.

Architect Eugene Kennedy, Jr. described the great edifice, handsomely decorated with mosaics and stained glass, as "a church for the ages." It overlooks the stone buildings of the surrounding campus of the Catholic University of America.

Down in the crypt you can view the jewel-studded tiara worn by Pope Paul VI at his coronation. In the same case is the gold-threaded stole worn by Pope John XXIII at the opening of Vatican Council 11 in 1962.

Mosaics of religious scenes in the Sacristy are the gifts of several Popes. The organs have a total of 9,138 pipes. Statistics on the exterior artwork are no less impressive. There are 200 pieces of sculpture and 137 statuary items all told.

The church was built in honor of Mary, whom a 19th century Pope proclaimed patron saint of the United States. Every year about one million pilgrims come here to pray. The first pontiff to visit Washington, D.C., Pope John Paul II, led morning prayers in this church on the Feast of the Holy Rosary.

Octagon House

1799 New York Ave. N.W., at corner of 18th St.

Tel: 638-3105. **Open:** 30 min. tours Tues.–Fri. 10 a.m.–4 p.m. Sat.–Sun. 1–4 p.m. **Admission:** Free. Metro station: Farragut West on Blue or Orange lines.

Just one block west of the White House is the city's oldest private mansion, an elegant brick building where President Madison lived for seven months after the British burned the White House.

On view in a circular second floor room is the desk upon which Madison signed the Treaty of Ghent in 1815, ending the last war between the United States and Britain.

No one knows why this building, shaped like a pregnant hexagon, came to be called the Octagon.

The wealthy Virginia plantation owner, Colonel John Tayloe, built it between 1798 and 1800 as a winter town house. His friend, George Washington, often rode over to watch it take shape.

Note how the architect, Dr. William Thornton, designed 13 curved doors to blend into the exact contours of the inside walls.

On view are British Regency chairs and a couch which belonged to the Tayloes.

There are fine examples of period furniture, including a striking pair of gilded wall mirrors in the drawing room. Among the distinguished visitors who sat in this room were Thomas Jefferson and the Marquis de Lafayette.

The basement level shows vaulted niches for wine bottles.

Changing exhibitions of architectural drawings are held as the building is owned by the American Institute of Architects Foundation.

Old Post Office Observatory

Pennsylvania Ave. between 11th & 12th Sts. N.W.

Tel: 523-5691. **Open:** Daily summer 8 a.m.–11 p.m., winter 10 a.m.–5 p.m. Every Thursday closed 6:30–9:30 p.m. **Admission:** Free. Gift shop & cafeterias. **Metro station:** Federal Triangle on Blue or Orange lines.

Once derided as "the old tooth" and slated for demolition, the renovated Old Post Office Building now offers the most spectacular overview of the nation's capital from atop its 315 ft. high tower. As a bonus draw there is the Pavilion, a sparkling mix of 50 shops, restaurants and performing arts center within the cavernous building.

A 47-second ride to the 9th floor in a glass-fronted elevator, and a change to another elevator for the ascent to the 12th floor, will make you feel on top of the world.

Below are the principal sights of Washington, D.C.: the domed Capitol and that stretch of Pennsylvania Avenue along which Presidents parade on Inauguration Day; the sleek Washington Monument; the gargantuan Pentagon and, also on the other side of the Potomac River, National Airport, with planes clearly visible as they land and take off.

Beyond the downtown offices and roof gardens, standing sentinel on the northwestern horizon, is the silhouette of Washington Cathedral. Also to the northwest, but only blocks away, is a portion of the gleaming White House.

Descend 71 steps down a spiral staircase and you'll arrive at the 10th floor repository for 10 bells—a Bicentennial gift to the U.S. Congress from the British Ditchley Foundation. The Congress Bells are rung when Congress opens and closes and on Federal holidays.

View over the Old Post Office Building

Pentagon

Southwest of Washington, D.C. across the Potomac River, in Va.

Tel: 695-1776. **Open:** Mon.–Fri. for one-hour tours at 9:30 a.m., 10 a.m., 11 a.m., 11:30 a.m., noon, 12:30 p.m., 1 p.m., 2 p.m., 2:30 p.m., 3:30 p.m. **Admission:** Free. Gift shop & cafeteria. **Metro station:** Pentagon on Blue or Yellow lines.

The headquarters of the Department of Defense would pass for a town in many countries. More than 23,000 people work here. It is so big that if the Washington Monument were laid flat on its side, from the outside wall facing in, it would not even reach the central courtyard around which the Pentagon's five sides are built.

Inside the building there are only five floors. But if all the corridors were joined together they would measure almost 18 miles long. There are 150 stairways, 19 escalators and 13 elevators.

You'd never guess that 25 percent of all the Pentagon's heating requirements for steam and hot water is provided by the daily burning of 10 tons of classified material.

Apart from the offices there are retail shops, department stores, drugstores, banks and even medical facilities, religious services and recreation areas.

Amazingly, this colossal building was constructed on reclaimed swamps. It was completed in 1943 after only 16 months work.

The 60 minute tours start less than half a minute's walk from the Pentagon Metrorail stop. You get the feel of the building's size and also rub shoulders with top military brass in the corridors.

In the Hall of Heroes are the names of the more than 3000 men and one woman who received the Medal of Honor.

State Department Diplomatic Reception Rooms

C & 22nd Sts. N.W.

Tel: 647-3241. **Open:** 45 minute tours Mon.–Fri. at 9:30 a.m., 10:30 a.m. & 3 p.m. **Admission:** Free. (Reservations should be made several weeks in advance though you can try your luck at filling cancellations). **Metro station:** Foggy Bottom on Blue or Orange lines, then 5-block walk south.

When the State Department was completed in 1961 the first dinner in the new rooms was planned for a reigning monarch. But the wife of the then Secretary of State reportedly wept when she looked upon the chrome, glass and concrete walls and tasteless furniture. It was then that Clement Conger, at that time deputy chief of protocol in charge of diplomatic entertainment, vowed to furnish the rooms in a style befitting the State Department.

What he assembled, entirely from donations and loans, has become one of the finest collections of Americana from about 1740–1830.

Visitors are taken to the three main diplomatic reception rooms, used daily for official functions.

The John Quincy Adams State Reception Room is furnished with Chippendale and has been called "the most beautiful American 18th century style drawing room in the country." Close by the fireplace is the mahogany table desk which Thomas Jefferson had in his Philadelphia apartment. The other desk is an English Sheraton Tambour on which Benjamin Franklin, John Jay and John Adams signed the Treaty of Peace with Britain in 1783.

The Thomas Jefferson State Reception Room is lit by an English cut glass Adam chandelier made about 1770.

The Benjamin Franklin State Dining Room has a horseshoe-shaped table seating 120 persons for state luncheons and dinners.

St. John's Church

Corner of 16th & H Sts. N.W.

Tel: 347-8766. **Open:** Daily 8 a.m.–5 p.m. **Admission:** Free. **Metro station:** McPherson Square or Farragut West on Blue or Orange lines.

This Episcopalian Church directly opposite the White House is also known as *The Church of the Presidents* because every President since James Madison worshipped in it.

A brass plate at pew 54 marks the place reserved for the President whenever he attends services here.

The church was designed in 1815 by Benjamin Latrobe, who wrote to his son: "I have just completed a church that made many Washingtonians religious who had not been religious before."

Latrobe, who designed parts of the Capitol and rebuilt the White House after the British torched it, was the first organist in this Greek Revival style building.

A stained-glass window in line with pew 54, and on the side closest to the White House, was donated by President Chester Arthur in memory of his wife. He asked for it to face the Executive Mansion so that he could look across Lafayette Square and see the light of the church shining through the window.

The adjacent *Parish House* at 1525 H Street was built in 1836 and was once owned by the editor of *The National Intelligencer,* the country's first national newspaper.

In 1842 the building became the residence of the British Minister, Lord Ashburton. In this house, in that same year, Ashburton and Secretary of State Daniel Webster signed the treaty establishing the border between the United States and Canada.

Supreme Court

Corner of 1st & East Capitol Sts. N.E.

Tel: 479-5000. **Open:** Mon.–Fri. 9:30 a.m.–3:30 p.m. Lecture in court every hour, on the half hour, 9:30 a.m.–3:30 p.m. when court not in session. **Admission:** Free. Gift shop & cafeteria. **Metro station:** Capitol South on Blue or Orange lines.

Nowhere else in America is tradition so strong and visible as within the Supreme Court of the United States.

The black-robed justices appear from behind parted red drapes as the Court Marshal announces: "The Honorable, the Chief Justice and the Associate Justices of the Supreme Court of the United States!"

As everyone remains standing, the crier continues: "Oyez! Oyez! Oyez! (Hear Ye!). All persons having business before the Honorable, the Supreme Court of the United States, are admonished to draw near and give their attention, for the Court is now sitting. God save the United States and this Honorable Court!"

The justices sit in seats of varying height, handcarved to their personal preference. The Chief Justice sits in the center of the winged bench. To his right sits the most senior Associate Justice. To his left the next senior, alternating left and right in order of seniority.

In this courtroom is another reminder of hallowed tradition. Ten-inch long white goose-quill pens are still placed on the lawyers' tables below the justices. Nowadays, after counsel have presented their 30 minute oral arguments, they take the quills home as souvenirs.

When the court sits it is in session every other fortnight, October–June, only on Mondays, Tuesdays and Wednesdays 10 a.m.–noon and 1–3 p.m.

Surratt House

604 H St. N.W., two blocks east of Convention Center.

John Wilkes Booth met in this former rooming house with fellow conspirators to plot the assassination of Abraham Lincoln.

Among the four convicted and executed was Mary Eugenia Surratt, the resident owner of the building who became the first woman hanged in the U.S.

Many historians now believe she was innocent and that she was convicted only because of circumstantial evidence.

Reverend Charles Stonestreet, testifying in her defense, said he had "always looked upon her as a proper Christian woman."

Booth was a frequent visitor to the house after becoming friendly with Mrs. Surratt's son, John, a clerk and a spy for the Confederacy.

The actual conspiracy was reportedly hatched in a parlor on the level below the attic of the eight-roomed house.

An entry in John Surratt's diary, six months before Booth shot Lincoln, stated: *"Booth wants his life but I shall oppose anything like murder."*

The building's outside appearance has changed since that calamitous April of 1865. Three nights after the assassination, law enforcement agents led the chubby, middle-aged Mrs. Surratt down the flight of wooden steps which used to lead off the main entrance at the present first floor.

The former basement is now the street level Chinese grocery shop. Rooms upstairs are privately occupied.

This area, in the heart of Chinatown, boasts the most pre-Civil War buildings between Capitol Hill and Georgetown.

U.S. Naval Observatory

34th & Massachusetts Ave. N.W.

Tel: 653-1543 (recorded information) or 653-1541 (further inquiries).
Open: Mondays only, Oct. 21–Apr. 27 at 7:30 p.m., Apr. 28–Oct.
20 at 8:30 p.m. **Admission:** Free. Guided tours 1½–2 hours. No
close metro station. Taxi or private car suggested.

Every Monday night 140 passes are issued on a
first-come-first-served basis for guided tours of the
only astronomical observatory in the U.S. that deter-
mines time.

Weather permitting, visitors get to peer through
the Observatory's largest telescope, a 26-inch refractor. It was the largest refractor in the world when an
astronomer looked through it in 1877 and discovered
Deimos and Phobos, the two moons of Mars.

The 1½–2 hour tour also leads to the 12-inch,
2000 pound refracting telescope and the Atomic
Clock, by which accurate time keeping is performed so
that the Observatory can determine standard time for
the United States.

The Observatory's six-inch and seven-inch transit
circles are used to measure the positions of thousands
of stars. This information, together with data on the
sun, moon and planets, is essential for safe navigation
in the air and at sea.

The Naval Observatory's 75,000 volume library,
in a rotunda room, is rated the best of its kind in the
nation, and includes 800 pre-19th century books.
However, it is open only to researchers at graduate
level and from government agencies.

Visitors should telephone 653-1543 before 5 p.m.
Mondays to find out if weather permits tours that
night. Children may join the tours but should have
some interest in or knowledge about the topic. Parking is outside the gate on 34th & Massachusetts
Avenue N.W. though the elderly and handicapped
may drive in.

Voice of America Studios

Independence Ave. S.W. between 3rd & 4th Sts.

Tel: 485-6231. **Open:** 35 min. guided tours Mon.–Fri. at 8:45, 9:45, 10:45 a.m., 1:45 & 2:45 p.m. **Admission:** Free. **Metro station:** Federal Center on Blue or Orange lines.

Here's a chance to see and listen in to one of the busiest radio newsroom studios in the world. From these headquarters of the Voice of America, news bulletins and feature programs on the American way of life are beamed in English and 41 other languages all over the world.

Journalists and technicians work shifts around the clock, telling the world about America 24 hours a day.

VOA ranks fourth in the world in the total number of hours of foreign language broadcasts beamed to other countries.

Your tour begins in front of the newsroom's glass screen. A row of clocks spells out time differences in every continent. Ticker tapes from the major wire services bring the editors up-to-date on breaking news.

Close by is the master control room where engineers tape reports filed in by VOA correspondents abroad. The television screens are used as back-ups to keep the news editors primed for hard news flashes.

The green buttons in the master control room show engineers the extent of jamming by hostile nations.

You'll see many glass-enclosed booths where newscasters sit before microphones reading the news.

Press a button and you'll hear the news in Uzbek, Lao, Hausa, Bulgarian, Bengali, Swahili or any of the other 41 languages. Programs are also beamed in a slow, special English for listeners with a limited English vocabulary.

Washington Cathedral

Northwest Washington, bounded by Massachusetts Ave., Wisconsin Ave. and Woodley Rd.

Tel: 537-6200. **Open:** Main floor, daily 10 a.m.–4:30 p.m. Rare Book Library, daily except Mon., noon–4 p.m. **Tours:** Mon.–Sat. 10 a.m.–noon, 1–3:15 p.m. Sun. 12:30–2 p.m. (hours subject to change). **Admission:** Free. Gift Shop. No close Metro station. Any of the Metrobuses with numbers in the 30s.

When the scheduled date for completion is reached in 1990 work on this Episcopal Cathedral will have taken 83 years, but it will be the sixth largest cathedral in the world.

The top of the *Gloria in Excelsis* tower is already the highest point in Washington at 676 ft. above sea level. It is one tenth of a mile from the west end of the nave to the high altar.

When President Theodore Roosevelt laid the foundation stone in 1907 he used the same silver trowel held by George Washington in setting the cornerstone of the Capitol.

Officially it is the Cathedral of St. Peter and St. Paul, but is widely known as National Cathedral.

The architecture is drawn from 14th century Gothic and the walls are made of Indiana limestone. Philip Hubert Frohman was the principal architect from 1921 until his death in 1972.

President Woodrow Wilson and his second wife, Edith, are entombed here.

Portraits of George Washington, by Gilbert Stuart and Rembrandt Peale, look down on many books from the 16th century in the *Rare Book Library*. A Book of Common Prayer, dated 1789, has a prayer of thanksgiving for religious and civil liberties, to be read every Fourth of July. A first edition of the King James Bible, printed in 1611, belonged to Henry, Prince of Wales.

White House

1600 Pennsylvania Ave. N.W. between West & East Executive Aves.

Tel: (tours) 456-7041. **Open:** 20-minute tours Tues.–Sat. 10 a.m.–noon. Everyone in line by noon will still get in. East Gate entrance. **Admission:** Free. Gift shop. **Metro station:** Farragut West or McPherson Square on Blue or Orange lines.

You don't have to be a VIP to enter the White House and perhaps see the President. Five of the 132 rooms are open to the public. And if you get on the VIP tour (your Member of Congress may have spare tickets, tel. 224-3121) you'll see even more, without having to wait in line.

George Washington died before its completion and remains the only President not to have lived in the White House.

His successor, John Adams, moved in with his wife, Abigail in November 1800. Thomas Jefferson, the third President, joked that the President's House was "big enough for two Emperors, one Pope and the Grand Lama."

The British burned the White House in 1814 but a freak thunderstorm doused the flames and saved the shell of sandstone walls.

Gas lighting was installed in 1848, the first elevator in 1882 and electricity in 1890. The President's famous Oval Office was built in 1909.

In 1948 the floors vibrated in President Truman's second floor study and the ceiling plaster sagged in the East Room. After the building was strengthened with concrete foundations and steel supports, the consulting engineer declared "the outer walls, which have stood for more than a century, will endure for centuries more."

The *East Room* is the largest of the state reception rooms. The full-length portrait of George Washington was saved by Dolley Madison in 1814, hours before the British burned everything inside.

Courtesy Washington Convention & Visitors Association

The White House, from the south lawn

The *Green Room* was Thomas Jefferson's dining room and thereafter a parlor room for small receptions.

The *Blue Room* is where the President brings Heads of State and other VIPs after welcoming them on the South lawn. They walk upstairs and enter the White House through the center glass door of this room.

The *Red Room* is often rearranged into a dining room.

The *State Dining Room* seats 140 people. Inscribed on the mantle below the fireplace are words written by President John Adams in 1800: "I pray Heaven to Bestow the Best of Blessings on This House and on All that shall hereafter inhabit it. May none but Honest and Wise Men ever rule under this roof."

Woodrow Wilson House

2340 S St. N.W.

Tel: 387-4062. **Open:** 45–60 min. guided tours Tues.–Sun. 10 a.m.–4 p.m. Closed January. **Admission:** Adults $2.50, children $1. Gift shop. **Metro station:** Dupont Circle on Red line then 7-block walk northwest up Massachusetts Ave.

Woodrow Wilson was the only President to live in the capital after his term expired and he stayed in this town house from the day he left the White House until his death three years later in 1924.

Though Edith Wilson had "discovered" the red-brick Georgian Revival house while scouting for a home, her husband gave her the keys as a surprise for their 5th wedding anniversary.

After his death, his widow lived on here until her own demise in 1961, when she bequeathed it to the nation.

The rooms have been kept as they were during the Wilson's occupancy. On view in his "dugout" is Wilson's 19th century typewriter, on which he typed his famous 14 Points for global stability after World War I.

In the large drawing room there's a mosaic of St. Peter given him by Pope Benedict XV. The library has a graphoscope (projector) which Douglas Fairbanks, Sr. gave Wilson so he could watch movies at home. Visitors pass through the solarium where the couple breakfasted overlooking their garden.

Upstairs in Wilson's bedroom is his huge bed, a replica of the Lincoln Bed he slept on in the White House. In Edith Wilson's bedroom is a wall painting of the Indian, Pocahontas, from whom she was a ninth generation descendant.

Many visitors believe the highlight of these rooms is the Wilson's clothes, displayed behind glass-faced closets.

MONUMENTS
AND MEMORIALS

The Jefferson Memorial

Arlington National Cemetery

Across the Potomac River, immediately after Memorial Bridge and Jefferson Davis Highway, in Va.

Tel: 692-0931. **Open:** Daily 8 a.m.–5 p.m., Apr. thru Sept. to 7 p.m. **Admission:** Free. Gift shop in Custis-Lee Mansion. **Metro station:** Arlington Cemetery on Blue line. Gray Line & Tourmobile routes.

Across the Potomac River, on the slopes of more than 1000 green acres of Virginia soil, lie the remains of Presidents John F. Kennedy, William Howard Taft and thousands of servicemen who fought at home and abroad from the Revolutionary to the Vietnam wars.

Here, too, are the graves of noted ex-servicemen, including Generals John Pershing, George Marshall and Omar Bradley, astronauts Roger Chafee and Virgil Grissom, former Secretary of State John Foster Dulles, ex-world heavyweight boxing champ Joe Louis, and Abraham Lincoln's son, Captain Robert Todd Lincoln.

One of the most moving experiences is to view the changing of the guard before the Tombs of the Unknown Soldiers, every hour on the hour.

Perched on the top of the hill is the Custis-Lee Mansion, built by George Washington Parke Custis, the adopted son of George Washington, between 1802 and 1817.

His daughter, Mary, lived here with her husband, the famed confederate military commander, Robert E. Lee, and their seven children.

In front of the mansion, overlooking the Federal capital he planned, is the tomb of Pierre Charles L'Enfant.

Tour buses with guides shuttle visitors from the parking lot to the gravesite of President Kennedy, the Tombs of the Unknown Soldiers and the Custis-Lee Mansion.

Jefferson Memorial

South bank of the Tidal Basin

Tel: 426-6821. **Open:** Daily. **Admission:** Free. Gift shops. No close Metro station. Gray Line and Tourmobile routes.

The white-domed, colonnaded building on the south bank of the Tidal Basin surrounds a 19 ft. high statue of Thomas Jefferson, third President of the United States and author of the Declaration of Independence.

The best time to visit is during late March or early April when thousands of Japanese cherry trees blossom with pink flowers around the Tidal Basin.

Another good time to go is at dusk in summer when the Marine Band serenades visitors sitting on the steps of the memorial.

Built on land reclaimed from the Potomac River, the memorial was dedicated in 1943, but only after a group of angry women chained themselves to an uprooted cherry tree to protest removal of the trees to make way for the monument. Only 83 trees were actually cut down while thousands more remained.

The bronze statue portrays Jefferson addressing the Continental Congress. It stands on a six foot high pedestal of black Minnesota granite.

Inscriptions on the interior walls of white Georgia marble are drawn from the best of Jefferson's texts. They are taken from the Declaration of Independence (*"We hold these truths to be self-evident"*), his Virginia Statute for Religious Freedom (*"Almighty God hath created the mind free"*), his belief in freedom from slavery (*"God who gave us life gave us liberty"*) and his opinions on the need for change in democracies (*"I am not an advocate for frequent changes"*).

Lincoln Memorial

On western end of the Mall, south of Constitution Ave. N.W.

Tel: 426-6895. **Open:** Daily 8 a.m.–midnight. **Admission:** Free. Gift shop. Light refreshments near base. No close Metro station. Gray Line & Tourmobile routes.

Washington's most imposing monument is a classically designed Grecian temple at the western end of the Mall. It honors the memory of Abraham Lincoln, 16th President of the United States.

This has been the focal point for some of the most stirring events in modern American history. In 1963 Dr. Martin Luther King, Jr. stood here before almost a quarter of a million people to deliver his famous *"I have a dream"* speech.

A few months later President Johnson led candle-carrying throngs in ceremonies marking the end of national mourning for John F. Kennedy.

The giant statue of a seated Lincoln is made of 28 blocks of white Georgia marble. If the sculpted President rose up he would stand 28 feet tall. Designed by Daniel Chester French, the statue rests on a pedestal of Tennessee marble.

To the left of the entrance is Lincoln's Gettysburg Address, one of the best speeches known to humankind. It was delivered at the dedication of a Civil War cemetery in Pennsylvania.

The chamber to the right of Lincoln's statue is inscribed with the words of his second inaugural address.

Lincoln's statue looks down upon the huge rectangular Reflecting Pool. In winter the frozen pool is a favorite with ice skaters.

The Lincoln Memorial

Marine Corps War Memorial (Iwo Jima Statue)

Outside northern border of Arlington Cemetery & U.S. 50. On Gray Line route.

The most famous photograph of World War II, snapped by AP newsphotographer Joe Rosenthal as U.S. Marines planted the Stars and Stripes atop Mt. Suribachi on Iwo Jima island, is reproduced as this bronze sculptural monument to all marines who gave their lives for the U.S. since 1775.

The 78 ft. high memorial by sculptor Felix W. de Weldon was dedicated by President Eisenhower in 1954 on the 179th anniversary of the U.S. Marine Corps. In 1961 President Kennedy decreed that a cloth flag fly from the memorial's 60 ft. high bronze flagpole 24 hours a day.

The memorial depicts the moment of triumph as five Marines and a Navy hospital corpsman raised the flag over the top of the extinct volcano, 660 miles south of Tokyo, on 23 February 1945. It was the crowning glory in the battle for the island, which claimed almost 23,000 marine casualties, including 5563 killed.

The sculptor faithfully depicted the likenesses of three of the six surviving flagbearers from life poses. The other three were later killed in action and their features were modeled from photographs.

The actual flag raised by the six combat troops can be viewed in the Marine Corps Museum at the Washington Navy Yard (see page 51).

At the base of the monument, etched in gold on the Swedish granite, are the names and dates of Marine Corps engagements over more than two centuries. Also inscribed is the tribute to the troops on Iwo Jima by Fleet Admiral Chester Nimitz: "Uncommon valor was a common virtue."

Vietnam Veterans Memorial

Constitution Gardens near Lincoln Memorial, between 21st & 22nd Sts. N.W.

Tel: 659-2490. **Open:** 24 hours daily. **Admission:** Free. **Metro station:** Foggy Bottom on Blue or Orange lines, then 8-block walk south on 23rd St. Gray Line and Tourmobile routes to nearby Lincoln Memorial.

Since its dedication in 1982, this memorial has become one of the most visited landmarks in the capital. Its black granite walls are gritblasted with the names of the more than 58,000 who gave their lives or who remain unaccounted for.

The walls were designed by Maya Ying Lin of Athens, Ohio, who was a 21-year-old senior at Yale University when she won the nationwide design competition in 1981. The bronze sculpture of three servicemen standing separate from the walls, but forming part of the memorial, is the work of Washington sculptor, Frederick Hart.

The two walls, each 246 ft. 8 in. long, are angled to enfold the Washington Monument and the Lincoln Memorial in a symbolic embrace with past history. Each wall has 70 upright panels of granite quarried near Bangalore, India.

The names are listed in the chronological order they became casualties, with the first of the fallen appearing on the top line of the East wall, at the point where the walls meet, under the date 1959. Successive listings continue on to the end of this wall and follow through from the lowest part of the west wall, so that the first and last casualties appear as the beginning and the end of the war at the point where the walls meet.

Diamond symbols next to a name denote confirmation of death. Symbolic crosses mean the serviceperson is missing.

Washington Monument

Western part of the Mall, south of Constitution Ave. N.W.

Tel: 426-6841. **Open:** Daily 9 a.m.–5 p.m. Apr.–Labor Day 8 a.m.–midnight. **Admission:** Free. Gift shop. **Metro station:** Smithsonian on Blue & Orange lines.

An elevator ride up the Washington Monument lifts visitors high above the Federal capital for a bird's-eye-view of the White House, the Pentagon and other landmarks in the city and neighboring Virginia and Maryland.

Since its completion in 1884 the marble obelisk has remained the world's tallest masonry structure, soaring 555 ft. 5 1/8 in. above its field of grass.

But it took 101 years to complete after the Continental Congress voted to honor George Washington.

The Monument rises in a straight line between the Capitol and the Lincoln Memorial but is off-center between the White House and the Jefferson Memorial because the original site was too marshy to build on.

The obelisk had reached about 150 feet in 1854 when masked men stole a block of Roman marble donated by Pope Pius IX. The stone was never recovered and may have been smashed and dumped into the Potomac River.

This incident, together with the Civil War, led to a drop in donations of marble and money and work on the Monument came to a halt. The stub of marble stood neglected for a quarter of a century until Congress approved funds for its completion.

The point at which work resumed is marked by the different coloring of the Maryland marble quarried from a different stratum in 1880. It was completed in 1884.

ART
GALLERIES

View over the National Gallery of Art

Corcoran Gallery of Art

Corner of 17th St. & New York Ave. N.W.

Tel: 638-3211. **Open:** Tues.-Sun. 10 a.m.-4:30 p.m. Thurs. until 9 p.m. **Admission:** Adults $1.50, children 50¢. Gift shop. **Metro station:** Farragut West on Blue or Orange lines then 5-block walk south on 17th St.

This stupendous collection of American and European art includes the famous portrait of George Washington by Gilbert Stuart, which is reproduced on all one dollar bills. There is also a giant painting of the old U.S. House of Representatives, done in 1822 by the same Samuel Morse who later invented Morse Code.

The banker/philanthropist, William Wilson Corcoran, had this colossus built in 1897 to show off his private collection which had grown too large for its original home in the Renwick Gallery.

More than a quarter century later, another wing was added to house the staggering collection of Senator William Clark, a farm boy who made millions from precious metals. Among the stunning exhibits is the *entire* Grand Salon from the Hotel D'Orsay in Paris, originally built for the Duc de la Tremouille during the 18th century reign of King Louis XVI. Clark had purchased this salon—complete with ceiling, walls and furniture—in 1904, and installed it in his New York City townhouse.

Moderns include Willem de Kooning and Vernon Fisher. Celebrated European artists are represented with works by, among others, Rembrandt Van Rijn, Gainsborough, Constable, J.W. Turner, Corot and Delacroix. Among fine examples by some early American portrait painters are canvases by Rembrandt Peale, Sully, Copley and Healey. Don't miss the delightful portrait in the Atrium of Benjamin Franklin, painted in 1782 by Joseph Wright.

Freer Gallery of Art

Jefferson Drive S.W. at 12th St.

Tel: 357-2700. **Open:** Daily except Christmas 10 a.m.–5:30 p.m.
Admission: Free. Gift Shop. **Metro station:** Smithsonian on Blue or
Orange lines.

The multi-millionaire railroad car manufacturer, Charles Lang Freer, donated so many Oriental and American art treasures to the nation that only about 8% of the 26,000 items can be shown at any one time. However, even this limited showing confirms it as one of the world's finest museums of Oriental art.

Freer's deep friendship with the artist, James McNeill Whistler, resulted in no less than two rooms being hung exclusively with his paintings. Don't miss the artist's portrait of Freer which was unfinished on Whistler's death in 1903. Freer said of this painting that Whistler was "making me look like a pope."

Highlighted in the granite and marble building, which Freer instructed his architect to design in the style of a Florentine renaissance palazzo, is the *Peacock Room.* Whistler had worked in oil and gold on leather and wood to create this extravaganza for the London mansion of Frederick Leyland. Freer bought it in 1904 and had it installed in his Detroit residence.

Lovers of Oriental art will be overjoyed at the display spanning more than four millenia of work in jade, bronze, pottery, silk, paper and lacquerware. There are round, decorated bronze Chinese mirrors, ancient jade rings, combs and pendants. Captivating 18th century Japanese handscrolls are meticulously decorated in ink, color and gold on paper and silk. The 17th century Japanese screens are no less exquisite.

Hirshhorn Museum & Sculpture Garden

Independence Ave., S.W. at 8th St.

Tel: 357-2700. **Open:** Daily except Christmas 10 a.m.–5:30 p.m. **Admission:** Free. Gift shop & plaza cafe. **Metro station:** Smithsonian on Blue or Orange lines.

Joseph Hirshhorn was only six when he arrived in the U.S. as a poor Latvian immigrant but by the time he died in 1981 he had become a business mogul with millions made from uranium mines. It enabled him to indulge his voracious passion for buying works of art which he amassed into one of the largest privately-held collections in any country. And he gave it all—4000 paintings and 2000 sculptures—as a gift to the nation.

The cylindrical structure is raised on pylons above the courtyard it encloses. Sculptures are in the inner circular walkways of the doughnut-shaped building. Paintings and drawings hang in outer galleries.

From the balcony of the third floor Abram Lerner Room, named after the museum's founding director, there is a sweeping overview of the Mall and of the Hirshhorn Sculpture Garden cut into it below ground level.

The museum boasts the largest public collection in the U.S. of sculpture by Henry Moore. There are many works by Rodin, Manzu, Matisse, Jacob Epstein, Picasso, Jacques Lipchitz, Houdon and Degas.

Of particular note are 14 bronze caricatures by Honoré Daumier, and a wood figure of a Polynesian goddess by Gaugin.

Picasso, Graham Sutherland, Jackson Pollock and de Kooning are represented among the prints, drawings and paintings. There are also large surrealist offerings by Salvador Dali, Tanguy and Magritte.

National Gallery of Art

Madison Drive between 3rd & 7th Sts. N.W.

Tel: 842-6188, 842-6190/1. **Open:** Sun. noon–9 p.m. Mon.–Sat. 10 a.m.–5 p.m. (summer hours may be extended). Closed Christmas & New Year's Day. **Admission:** Free. Gift shop & cafeteria. **Metro station:** Judiciary Square on Red line, Archives on Yellow line or Smithsonian on Blue or Orange lines.

Among its stupendous collection of old masters and great moderns, the National Gallery of Art has the distinction of possessing the only painting in America by Leonardo da Vinci, and the single surviving set of portraits by Gilbert Stuart of the first five Presidents of the United States. In 1985 it paid a record auction price for an American painting in a successful bid of $3.7 million for Rembrandt Peale's portrait of *Rubens Peale with a Geranium*.

The older West Building, opened in 1941, is connected to the East Building, opened in 1978, by an open-air plaza and underground concourse with cafe, buffet, bookshop and souvenir facilities.

Gallery 6 in the West Building houses the painting by Leonardi da Vinci of the young Florentine girl, Ginevra de'Benci. Completed about 1474 it shows her against a background of a juniper bush. Paintings on this side of the Rotunda include masterpieces by Flemish, German and Dutch painters.

Gilbert Stuart's portraits of the first five Chief Executives are in Gallery 60B, to the right of the Rotunda. Stuart painted this set in Boston between 1805 and 1828.

Besides the American School, this side of the West Building contains an enviable collection of French impressionists and post-impressionists.

The East Building has a room full of paintings by Picasso.

National Museum of African Art

324 A St. N.E.

Tel: 357-2700. **Open:** Daily except Christmas, Mon.-Fri. 11 a.m.-5 p.m. Sat.-Sun. noon-5 p.m. **Admission:** Free. Gift shop. **Metro station:** Capitol South on Blue or Orange lines.

Of all the Smithsonian Museums, this one, a five minute walk behind the U.S Capitol, is located in the most historic home. In the 1870s it was the residence of the celebrated former slave, Frederick Douglass, who also owned the adjacent townhouse.

Douglass had fled from bondage when he was about 21, yet long before his death in 1895 he had become one of the most famous blacks in the U.S., renowned as a powerful orator and impassioned newspaper publisher championing abolition, the first black U.S. Marshal in the District of Columbia, Recorder of Deeds for D.C., and U.S. Minister to Haiti.

The permanent collection of African arts and crafts, though small in number in relation to other Smithsonian museums, nevertheless highlights the deftness of the rural African sculptors.

A notable exhibit from Benin City is a 16th century ivory spoon with a bird fashioned on the handle, all carved from an elephant's tooth. Equally arresting is a Sudanese clay-fired and pigmented pipe bowl in the shape of a hyena.

There are elaborate Sudanese hats, stitched with glass beads, animal hide and human hair; hammered gold earrings with red floss embroidery and incised designs from Mali; and a milk gourd decorated with glass beads and shells from Kenya.

The topmost floor contains many items associated with Douglass, including a first edition of the earliest of his three autobiographies, published in 1845.

National Portrait Gallery & National Museum of American Art

8th & G Sts. N.W.

Tel: 357—2700. **Open:** Daily except Christmas 10 a.m.–5:30 p.m.
Admission: Free. Gift shop & cafeteria. **Metro station:** Gallery Place
on Red or Yellow lines.

Both collections are exhibited in the same massive former U.S. Patent Office, which covers two full city blocks. The same building was a hospital during the Civil War and the scene of Abraham Lincoln's second inaugural ball.

The National Portrait Gallery is a visual reminder of Who Was Who in American politics and the arts and sciences. Among the most famous works here is the *Lansdowne* portrait of George Washington, painted by Gilbert Stuart in 1796.

The same artist took 16 years to deliver the finished portrait on view of Thomas Jefferson, even though the third President had paid him $100 for it at the outset.

Prominent among the portraits of Chief Executives in the *Hall of Presidents* is an extraordinarily crafty portrayal of Richard Nixon by Norman Rockwell.

In the *Gallery of Notable Americans* you'll find likenesses of Harriet Beecher Stowe, Henry Longfellow, Pocahontas, and a self-portrait of George Healy, who painted about 100 portraits a year and whose output is extensively represented in this building.

The gallery devoted to *Science & Invention* has the original automatic telegraph receiver patented by Samuel F.B. Morse in 1837. Close by is a portrait of the prosperous-looking Isaac Singer, inventor of the Singer sewing machine.

Among the many photographs of 19th century celebrities in the Meserve Gallery is the striking last life portrait of Abraham Lincoln, taken by Alexander Gardner just four days before his assassination.

Grouped together in another room are some of the titans of American industry: a plaster bust of John D. Rockefeller and portraits of Cornelius Vanderbilt, John Pierpont Morgan, and Andrew Carnegie who said a man should spend the first half of his life acquiring riches and the latter half distributing them.

Move on to the bronze cast of Phineas T. Barnum, founder of the circus billed as "the greatest show on earth", and then see the oils of Admiral Byrrd, first flight commander over the North and South Poles, and Amelia Earhart, the first woman to fly solo across the Atlantic.

There are excellent canvases by John Singleton Copley, Thomas Sully, Charles Wilson Peale, George Healy and Rembrandt Peale in the National Museum of American Art.

Particularly vivid are the series of paintings of Native Americans by George Catlin, and a bronze sculpture of a mounted warrior, *The Scalp,* by Frederic Remington.

OAS Headquarters & Museum of Modern Art of Latin America

Corner of 17th St. N.W. & Constitution Ave.

Tel: Museum 789-6016. **Open:** Tues.–Sat. 10 a.m.–5 p.m. **Admission:** Free. **Metro station:** Federal Triangle or Farragut West on Blue or Orange lines.

A triple treat awaits visitors just three blocks southwest of the White House. On one extended block is the handsome secretariat building of the Organisation of American States, the Aztec Garden and the flamboyant paintings and sculptures in the Museum.

Inside the gleaming white Georgia marble headquarters building is a Spanish colonial *patio,* complete with marble fountain, decorated tiled floors and the luxuriance of tropical trees reaching to the glass roof. Note the plaque on one tree planted in 1910 by President Taft.

At the top of the ceremonial stairs, flags of member states hang over busts of the continent's most famous liberators and heroes. Behind the 12 ft. high doors is the *Hall of the Americas,* with Ionic-topped columns, shimmering chandeliers and a high, vaulted ceiling. The windows look down on the large *Aztec Garden* with reflecting pool, sculptures and mosaics.

It is enclosed at the far end by the Museum of Modern Art of Latin America (entrance on 18th St.), created by the OAS in tribute to the bicentennial of U.S. independence. The Spanish-style building has a red-tiled roof, white walls, iron grilles and a decorated loggia facing the Aztec Garden. Constructed in 1912 with funds from Andrew Carnegie, it was the residence of OAS Directors & Secretaries General. Three floors are brought to brilliance with art from Latin America and the Caribbean.

Phillips Collection

1600 21st St. N.W. near Q St.

Tel: 387-2151. **Concert information** 387-0961. **Open:** Tues.–Sat. 10 a.m.–5 p.m. Sun 2–7 p.m. **Admission:** Free. Gift shop & cafeteria. **Metro station:** Dupont Circle on Red line.

Shortly after Duncan Phillips paid $125,000 in 1923 for Renoir's *Luncheon of the Boating Party,* an English nobelman handed him a blank check. "Fill in any amount and I will pay it," said Lord Joseph Duveen, who wanted it for the National Gallery in London. Phillips declined, for it was a prized possession, which he himself rated "one of the greatest pictures of the world."

Ever since, the painting, known in French as *Dejeuner des Canotiers,* has been the most prominent painting in an already marvelous collection assembled by Phillips and his wife Marjorie.

Phillips, who was a grandson of James Laughlin, banker and cofounder of the Jones & Laughlin Steel Company, purchased a treasure trove of works by 19th and 20th century French and American artists. Among those exhibited are works by Van Gogh, Chagall, Degas, Dufy, Braque, Rouault, Kokoschka, Renoir, Daumier, Cezanne, Bonnard and Klee.

Duncan Phillips wanted the public to "feel at home with the pictures in an unpretentious domestic setting." In 1930 he moved out of the Georgian Revival style mansion near Dupont Circle to make over even more room for the art treasures. A new wing was added in 1960.

Apart from the permanent collection, there are changing exhibitions of photographs, drawings, paintings and lithographs.

Free Sunday concerts are held in the music room September through May 5–7 p.m. Admission is free.

Renwick Gallery

Corner of Pennsylvania Ave. N.W. & 17th St.

Tel: 357-2700. **Open:** Daily except Christmas 10 a.m.–5:30 p.m. **Admission:** Free. Gift Shop. **Metro station:** Farragut West on Blue or Orange lines.

At the head of a majestic staircase, in a room appropriately known as *The Grand Salon,* is a full-length contemporary painting of the 19th century banker/philanthropist, William Wilson Corcoran. He was the fabulously wealthy Washingtonian who wrote his grandchildren: "The most valuable bequest I can make you is a good name."

Corcoran commissioned this magnificent structure to display his considerable art and sculpture collection to the public. Architect James Renwick based his design on the French Second Empire style after seeing the new addition to the Louvre in Paris.

The red-brick landmark was a Union hospital and then a supplies store during the Civil War.

In 1897 the burgeoning collection moved to larger premises, at its present site on 17th & New York Ave. N.W. The Renwick building became the Court of Claims for the next 65 years. Forlorn and aging, it was slated for demolition. Only its historic past and architectural significance won it a reprieve and today it is part of the Smithsonian's National Museum of American Art.

Changing exhibitions are staged of fine American decorative arts, crafts and design in metal, wood, glass, ceramics and fiber.

Permanent exhibits in *The Grand Salon* and *Octagon Room*, furnished in the style of the 1860s and 1870s, include 19th century porcelain vases from Sevres, France, and 18th and 19th century paintings by American, British, French and Spanish artists.

Out-Of-The-Ordinary Tours

Free guided tours are conducted through the downtown home of one of the nation's most influential and prestigious newspapers, *The Washington Post.*

Visitors are led through the news and press rooms to see various stages in the production of the daily paper at its downtown address, 1150 15th Street N.W. N.W.

Groups are advised to make advance reservations for this half hour tour, held Mondays through Fridays. Individuals without advance reservations may try their luck squeezing in on the daily tours, held every hour beginning at 10 a.m. and concluding after the 3 p.m. tour. Accompanying children must be at least 5th Graders.

For further information telephone 334-7969.

The annual *Georgetown House Tour,* sponsored by St. John's Episcopal Church, 3240 O Street N.W., is held every Spring. This is a unique opportunity to see the interiors of more than a dozen of the capital's architecturally splendid homes.

The walking tour is spread over two days in late April and the admission charge includes high tea at the church.

For further information telehone 338-1796.

Nationally-known celebrities are among the dozen or so homeowners who open their gates for the annual *Georgetown Garden Tour,* also in April.

The full-day tour, for which a charge is made, includes tea at the Georgetown Children's House, a day-care center for children of low-income working parents, and beneficiary of proceeds from the tour.

For further information telephone 338-4229.

The city's leading sightseeing organization, Gray Line, operates a *Black Heritage Tour* for groups chartering the motor-coaches.

Some of the highlights of this innovative 4 hour tour include stopovers at the Frederick Douglass Home (see page 72), the Museum of African Art (see page 106), a statue of Abraham Lincoln financed by freed slaves, the 56 ft. long mural in oils on the life of Dr. Martin Luther King, Jr., homes of prominent blacks and the birthplace of "Duke" Ellington.

For further information telephone 479-5900.

The annual *Embassy Tour,* which the First Lady traditionally chairs in an honorary capacity, is indisputably one of the year's most eagerly-awaited local events. When the Goodwill Industries Guild sponsored the first tour in 1947, invitations were sent out and those who accepted wore hats and gloves and paid at the door. Nowadays, even though all tickets are sold in advance, some years see more than 3000 persons on the tour.

The visit to about half a dozen embassies is always held on the second Saturday in May and generally lasts about six hours. Rides between the embassies are made on free shuttle buses. Refreshments are served and those on the tour get to meet distinguished guests, who traditionally include spouses of Ambassadors, Supreme Court Justices, Cabinet officers, chiefs of the Armed Forces, Congresspersons and other prominent Washingtonians.

For further information telephone 636-4225.

Sightseeers unable to make the tour should drive past a few embassies, if only because these elegant buildings were once the private homes of some of Washington's wealthiest and most colorful personalities. In particular, try and see:

Mexican Embassy, 2829 16th Street N.W. Believe it or not, this was built in 1911 as a surprise Christmas present from Nellie MacVeagh to her husband, Franklin, Treasury Secretary under President Taft. British Prime Minister, Arthur Balfour, and the King and Queen of Belgium were among distinguished house guests. Mexico purchased the building 10 years after the Christmas wrapping came off.

Georgetown

This northwestern slice of the District of Columbia boasts some of the ritziest homes, the quaintest boutiques and the widest listing of restaurants. There is an invigorating mix of bohemian drift and artistic drive.

Georgetown has been a fashionable place to live since John Kennedy moved to 3307 N Street before his election as President. After his assassination Jacqueline Kennedy returned to Georgetown, living for a while at 3017 N Street. In the area bounded by S Street, the canal, Rock Creek Park and Georgetown University, elegant hostesses preside over soirées for the cream of the diplomatic and political worlds.

Today Georgetown throbs with a seductive vitality. Young and old swarm along M Street and Wisconsin Avenue from dusk to the wee hours of the morning. This is particularly so in the weekends when private parking is hard to find.

Shoppers along M Street, Wisconsin Avenue and the side streets will find arts and crafts hideaways, design centers, antiques, clogs and candles, imported dresses, crewel and needlework, a shopfull of kites, patchwork quilts and hand-dyed yarns, art galleries, wall-hangings, books, records and old prints.

Some other notable Georgetown landmarks, in addition to the historic, but private homes mentioned above:

Old Stone House: 3051 M Street. Tel: 426-6851. A pre-Revolutionary structure built in 1765 and maintained by the National Park Service. Open: Wed.–Sun. 9:30 a.m.–5 p.m.

Dumbarton Oaks: 3101 R Street. Tel: 338–8278. 19th century mansion with collection of Byzantine jewelry and pre-Columbian art. Formal gardens. Open daily 2–5 p.m. See page 47.

ZOO, AQUARIUM PARKS AND GARDENS

Giant Pandas at the Zoo

National Aquarium

Department of Commerce Building, Pennsylvania Ave. N.W. at 14th St. entrance.

Tel: 377-2826 (recorded information) or 377-2825 (further inquiries). **Open:** Daily except Christmas 9 a.m.–5 p.m. **Admission:** Adults $1, Children 50¢. Gift shop & cafeteria. **Metro station:** Federal Triangle on Blue or Orange lines.

The best time to visit this oldest public aquarium in the U.S. is at 2 p.m. on any day except Friday.

At this time, on Mondays, Wednesdays and Saturdays, the lemon and nurse sharks are fed.

The deadly piranhas are fed at the same time on Tuesdays, Thursdays and Sundays.

Unlike octopi, which feed almost exclusively on live crabs and small fish, the sharks and piranhas devour almost anything dropped in their tanks.

About 1000 specimens from salt and fresh water, representing some 200 different species, are in 63 display tanks. There are Moray and electric eels, a sea turtle and even a live alligator.

A special *Touch Tank* holds crabs, sea urchins, conches and other live sea creatures that even children may handle.

The free mini-theater presents a 15-minute slide show about aquatic life.

Founded in 1873, the National Aquarium is now operated by the private, non-profit National Aquarium Society.

It is located in the basement of the Department of Commerce building, which also houses the Visitor Information Center facing Pennsylvania Avenue. This gigantic building stretches over an entire extended block.

National Arboretum

440 acres in Northeast Washington, bounded by New York Ave., Bladensburg, Rd., and M. St. Entrance on New York Ave.

Tel: 475-4815. **Open:** Daily except Christmas Mon.–Fri. 8 a.m.–5 p.m. Sat.–Sun. 10 a.m.–5 p.m. **Bonsai Collection** 10 a.m.–2:30 p.m. **Admission:** Free. Gift Shop.

A car is essential to cover the nine miles of paved roads leading to the major plant groups in the 440 acres.

The National Bonsai Collection, valued at almost $5 million, is housed in a separate pavilion. These 53 miniature trees, wired and regularly pruned to keep their shape and dwarf stature, were a Bicentennial gift from the Japanese to the American people.

There are 34 different species, ranging in age from 30 to 350 years. A 180-year-old Japanese Red Pine from the Imperial household, represents the first time a bonsai from the royal collection has left Japan.

There are also several bonsai from King Hassan of Morocco.

Next to this sensational attraction is the National Herb Garden, spread over two acres. There are herbs from around the world, including native plants used in colonial times, herbs used in modern medicine, as food seasoners, for their fragrance, or even as sources of fuel, oil, pesticides and fibers.

The Gotelli collection of dwarf and slow-growing conifers adds up to some 1500 specimens, with many firs, cedars, false cypresses, junipers, spruce, pines, yews and hemlock dotted over five acres.

The extensive azalea plantings are among the largest in the nation and are the highlight of the spring profusion of color when they bloom from late April for a month. This is also the season to view the blooming rhodedendrons.

National Zoological Park

3001 Connecticut Ave. N.W.

Tel: 673-4800. **Open:** Daily, buildings 9 a.m.–4:30 p.m., grounds 8 a.m.–6 p.m. **Admission:** Free. Gift shop and cafeteria. **Metro station:** Woodley Park-Zoo on Red line, then short walk north up Connecticut Ave.

The main attraction among more than 3000 animals, reptiles and birds is a pair of Giant Pandas, Hsing-Hsing and Ling-Ling, donated by the People's Republic of China. Only about 1000 of these fluffy black and white pandas remain wild in the mountainous terrain of south central China. At each of their regular feeding times, 11 a.m. and 3 p.m., they consume more than 20 lbs. of food with a bamboo staple.

Six trails of painted footprints guide visitors to specific species in these 175 acres.

The Reptile House is among the more popular stops, with venomous snakes and several alligators. Adjacent, along the same Lion Trail, is the Great Ape House, where highly-expressive gorillas steal the show.

Try to stop in at the Elephant House at 2 p.m. to catch the special training demonstrations, when the large-eared African elephants and their smaller Indian cousins are put through their paces. The Elephant House is also home to the not-so-well-known pygmy hippopotami.

Free maps with the six trails are given out at information desks in the Education Building just inside the entrance.

Also here are regular free screenings of films about the Zoo's animal population. Here, too, is *Zoolab,* where visitors can see and touch skulls, antlers and feathers to learn more about the animal world. A similar *Birdlab* is in the Bird House along the Crowned Crane Trail.

Theodore Roosevelt Island

Accessible only from northbound lane of George Washington Memorial Parkway on Virginia side of Potomac River. Footbridge leads from parking lot to island.

Tel: 426-6922 or (703) 557-8990. **Open:** Daily 9:30 a.m.–sunset.

If you feel the need to break away from summer's crush of people and traffic then head for the middle of the Potomac River, opposite the Kennedy Center, to an idyllic 88-acre island retreat.

The island, accessible by footbridge from the parking lot on the Virginia shoreline, is a fitting memorial to a vigorous nature conservationist, President Theodore Roosevelt.

Here, along 2½ miles of quiet foot trails, are swamps, marshes and forest. It is a haven for marsh wren, kingfishers, turtles, squirrels, white cottontails and other protected animal life living among the willows, maples, elms and oaks.

On the northern portion of the island, which Britain's King Charles I granted to Lord Baltimore, is a 17 ft. high bronze statue of Roosevelt, sculpted by Paul Manship.

The 26th President stands against a backdrop of a 30 ft. high granite shaft overlooking an oval terrace. Four granite tablets, each 21 ft. high, are inscribed with Roosevelt's beliefs, in his own words, on Nature, Manhood, Youth and the State.

"There is delight in the hardy life of the open," said Roosevelt, whose administration established the U.S. Forest Service, five National Parks, 51 bird refuges and four game refuges.

Congress approved funds for the permanent memorial in 1963 and formal dedication ceremonies were held in 1967.

U.S. Botanic Garden

Southwest Washington, at junction of 1st St., Maryland Ave. & Independence Ave.

Tel: 225-7099. **Open:** Daily except Christmas 9 a.m.–5 p.m. **Admission:** Free. **Metro station:** Federal Center on Blue or Orange lines.

The glass and aluminum conservatory bulging up at the right foot of the west front of the Capitol is a year-round extravaganza in green.

A total of 9000 sq. ft. of exhibition halls are scented with the rarest of plants native to tropical, subtropical and desert climates. Many of the trees and ferns originate in Brazil and other South American countries, where the popular imagery of lush plant life is borne out by a visit here.

There are cacti from Africa that would not look out of place in the American southwest. Among seasonal specials are tulips, gladioli, chrysanthemums and poinsettias. All told, there are more than 8000 species and varieties.

Though green predominates, the multi-hued orchids, strongly fragrant, bloom by the score every week. They have for years enjoyed a world-wide reputation for variety and perfection.

There are also magnificent groups of aroids, bromeliads, cycads, ferns and palms, fulfilling the initial goal set by Congress when establishing the Botanic Garden in the mid-19th century, "...to collect, cultivate and grow the various vegetable production of this and other countries for exhibition and display..."

Directly across Independence Avenue is a garden featuring summer blooming annuals, bulbs and perennials. The large and impressive fountain was conceived by Frederic Bartholdi, best known for his design of the Statue of Liberty.

Children's Specials

Apart from the museums, zoo, aquarium and other attractions mentioned elsewhere in this book, there are a variety of exciting diversions for restless young children in captive tow.

On the Mall, near the Smithsonian "Castle", there's all the fun of the fairground aboard the gaily-decorated *carousel.*

Inside the Mall museums there are special children's activities. At the Arts & Industries Building, close to the carousel, there are delightful live theatrical performances in the *Discovery Theater.* Geared to children from pre-kindergarten to 8th Grade, the shows are 45–60 minutes long and are held Tues.–Fri. 10 & 11:30 a.m. and Sat. at 1 & 3 p.m. Admission: Adults $3, children 12 & under $2.50.

Across the other side of the Mall, in the second floor of the National Museum of Natural History, there is a *Discovery Room* where children of all ages can see, touch, smell and taste a wide sampling of natural history specimens. Open: Mon.–Thurs. noon–2:30 p.m. Fri.–Sun. 10:30 a.m.–3:30 p.m.

Across the Ellipse, near the White House, young children will thrill to the sight of antique dolls and toys in the *Children's Attic* of the Daughters of the American Revolution Museum. There is also a *touch program* in which concealed objects are guessed at (see page 44).

A visit to the *Capital Children's Museum* at 800 3rd Street N.E. (Tel: 543-8600), behind Union Station, is perhaps the funnest experience for younger children from pre-kindergarten to about Grade 5. Kids play at using communications equipment, such as telephones and computers, and there are myriad other hands-on learning devices. They can participate in craft workshops by, for example, making a pinata or operating a printing press. Open: Tues.–Sat. 10 a.m. -

4 p.m. Sun. 1–5 p.m. Admission: $2 per person.

Pedal boating on the Tidal Basin in front of the Jefferson Memorial is a popular summer pastime for family groups. Boats are hired for 30–60 minutes from the pier northeast of the Memorial, not far from the 15th Street exit of the Bureau of Engraving & Printing.

Most children delight in seeing and listening to military bands. They perform June through August at 8 p.m. at the Sylvan Theater, near the Washington Monument on Sun., Tues., Thurs., Fri. and at the U.S. Capitol west terrace on Mon., Tues., Wed., Fri. (Tel: 426-6700).

At the Washington Navy Yard, a 7 minute drive southeast of the Capitol, children can join the free 30 minute guided tours of a decommissioned *Destroyer.* The 424 ft. long *USS Barry* took part in the quarantine of Cuba during the 1962 missile crisis and saw combat in Vietnam. Open: 10 a.m.–4 p.m. (Tel: 433-2651).

A huge collection of Victorian dolls houses, toys and games awaits interested children and even nostalgic adults at the *Dolls' House & Toy Museum* near the Friendship Heights Metro station on the Red line (see page 46).

Further out, about 35 minutes by car, is the *National Capital Trolley Museum.* The admission fee of $1 for adults and 75¢ for children, includes entry to the fine collection of antique American and European trolleys and streetcars, and a ride on one of them. Open: Memorial–Labor Days noon–5 p.m., rest of the year until 4 p.m. It is located at Bonifant Road, between Layhill Road and New Hampshire Avenue, north of Wheaton, Md. From downtown Washington, drive north up New Hampshire Avenue N.W. (Route 650) until it abuts Bonifant Road, then turn left. (Tel: 384-9797).

Alexandria, Va.

Only 11 minutes south of Washington by Metrorail, this is an historic city, where George Washington frequently worshipped and where Robert E. Lee spent his formative years. It was surveyed as a town as far back as 1749 and some of the streets are still surfaced with old cobblestones.

The clipper ships which sailed to this third busiest port in the colonies, are gone, but the waterfront is as vibrant. A former U.S. Navy factory, which made torpedo shell cases, is now the bustling Torpedo Factory Art Center where some 200 artists can be seen at work while their ceramics, paintings and sculptures are up for sale.

There is a profusion of quaint 18th and 19th century houses, many of which have been converted into shops, museums or public service offices. The *Ramsay House Visitors' Center,* at 221 King St., was built in 1724 and was the home of the merchant and city founder, William Ramsay. Next door is *Carlyle House*, a mid-18th century Georgian mansion where a British general met with five colonial governors to discuss taxation without representation.

George Washington's pew is preserved at *Christ Church,* where Robert E. Lee was confirmed. In the grounds of the *Old Presbyterian Meeting House,* built in 1774, stands the Tomb of the Unknown Soldier of the American Revolution.

Robert E. Lee's Boyhood Home is now filled with antiques and Lee memorabilia. There is a colonial style restaurant in *Gadsby's Tavern,* from whose steps Washington reviewed the Alexandria Independent Infantry Blues in 1798. Among the many other historic buildings to be seen is the *George Washington National Masonic Memorial.* An elevator ride more than 100 yards up provides a panoramic view of the surroundings, including the capital.

INDEX